AS WE BEGIN

Dispositions of Mind,
Learning, and the Brain in
Early Childhood

Tia Henteleff

FROM HODDER EDUCATION

Orders: please contact Hachette UK Distribution, Hely Hutchinson Centre, Milton Road, Didcot, Oxfordshire, OX11 7HH. Telephone: +44 (0)1235 827827. Email education@hachette.co.uk. Lines are open from 9 a.m. to 5 p.m., Monday to Friday.

ISBN: 9781398369436

© Tia Henteleff 2023

First published in 2023 by
John Catt from Hodder Education,
An Hachette UK Company
15 Riduna Park, Station Road,
Melton, Woodbridge IP12 1QT
Telephone: +44 (0)1394 389850
www.johncatt.com

MIX
Paper | Supporting responsible forestry
FSC
www.fsc.org
FSC™ C104740

In memory of Elliot W. Eisner whose teaching and mentorship continues to light my path.

Dedicated to my family who are always teaching, inspiring, and lifting me up, Jonah, Stella, Sheldon, Owen, and Eli.

Instructions for living a life.
Pay attention.
Be astonished.
Tell about it.

Mary Oliver

There is perhaps no more important time in a human's development than their childhood, and after the family, there are perhaps no more important people to a child than educators. This book is an informative foray into just how important you, readers, are. Indulge, enjoy, and learn.

Mary Helen Immordino-Yang, Professor of Education, Psychology and Neuroscience

Foundations for a child's learning and academic, social and emotional development are set in their earliest years of schooling. *As We Begin* elevates how we think and design for our youngest learners' brains by sharing research and strategies that will validate and transform early childhood education and educators.

Glenn Whitman, executive director of The Center for Transformative Teaching and Learning and co-author of Neuroteach

Teaching primary learners is a role that requires patience, skill, exceptional caring, and the understanding of how learning occurs for our youngest students. In *As We Begin: Dispositions of Mind, Learning, and the Brain in Early Childhood*, Tia Henteleff uses her expertise and experience as a primary educator to unpack the importance of Mind, Brain, and Education science as a lever for elevating teaching practice in early childhood education. It is going to help a lot of educators.

Margaret Lee, educator, consultant, & author of Mindsets for Parents

A delightful read that strikes the perfect balance between personal story and research on how young children learn and grow. This book is for educators, researchers, parents, and everyone invested in children. If you are an educator, Henteleff's prose will reaffirm your choice and your essential work in laying the foundations of the future. Researchers will find new importance in their work and motivation to continue to understand the nature of young children's minds. Parents will find affirmation and awe in the importance of the beginning. Because, as Henteleff powerfully states, the beginning does not just matter during the beginning. Early childhood sets the stage for everything to come. *As*

We Begin is friendly and accessible, yet deeply meaningful. Henteleff is genuine and her passion for children and educators is tangible in every word. This is truly a book for everyone and a must-read for educators, parents, and researchers!

Kristin Gagnier, senior research scientist

Thoughtful and practical, *As We Begin* cuts through the noise to center us on what really matters in early childhood education – relationships, emotions, creativity, curiosity, and growth. Henteleff brings together the best of cutting-edge interdisciplinary research, illuminating theory, and traditional and progressive educational approaches, to provide a much-needed teacher/researcher perspective on the field of Mind, Brain, and Education. She offers powerful ideas for all those seeking to improve the ways we support students' learning.

Rebecca Gotlieb, human developmental psychologist and educational neuroscientist

CONTENTS

FOREWORD

A note to the reader

While this book was written with early childhood educators in mind, it will be useful for educators of any age, as well as parents, and anyone that is interested in ideas and research surrounding curiosity, creativity, brain development, and learning. These topics are fascinating (even astonishing at times), incredibly important, and pertinent to … everyone.

To the educators

Thank you for what you do. You have chosen a career to help others and that work presents new, multi-faceted, and idiosyncratic challenges with each new day. Many of those challenges impact individuals whose faces you can picture in your mind right now, people that you know well and care deeply about whether it be children you have worked with in the past or present, families you have gotten to know, or colleagues you have worked beside. We, in the field of education, are on an important and interesting journey where upcoming bends, hills, plains, and cliffs are not always predictable and yet our work has impact beyond what we can see.

Teaching is rooted in the past but seeks growth and transformation in the present and future. Knowledge of the past gives us the information needed in the present to facilitate brain change, growth, and the development of rewarding relationships. Teaching is about making the most out of the moment we have right now, learning and growing within that moment for whatever it affords us. However, with an eye to the future, teachers also consciously decide what, how, and why we teach in order to have a positive impact on the future of each student. And while this may be a cliche, the act of teaching is an investment of time, energy, and money in children as well as our collective future on this planet.

This is a profession that seeks to make lives better, that seeks to understand and solve problems, and this is a profession that necessitates phenomenal amounts of hard work, intelligence, courage, patience, and heart.

So again, thank you!

PART 1:
THE BIG IDEAS

THE BEGINNING

Beginnings hold power and promise for what is to come; this is equally true of the beginning of a book, the beginning of a life, or the beginning of school. We cannot be certain of what is to follow, but we do understand that beginnings are often singular and memorable moments that introduce us to the story that is about to unfold. As Plato said about childhood education in *The Republic*, 'the beginning is the most important part of the work'. Early childhood is the beginning of life. Early childhood education is the beginning of a relationship with teachers, with schools, and with learning communities. It is the promise of a positive association with learning, education, and one's potential. Most early childhood educators know this, and this is why we feel passionate about what we do.

The beginning does not just matter during the beginning.

The beginning matters to everything that comes next.

I will keep returning to the importance of early childhood learning and education. That is what drew me into teaching and is what compelled me to write this book. We, as early childhood educators, have an awesome job, one that comes with many intrinsic responsibilities and rewards. As if teaching children during these years at the beginning of their relationships with peers, teachers, and compulsory education was not enough, these are also important years of brain development. At this time the creativity, imagination and intellectual curiosity of children is endlessly fascinating. And if they do not already possess a disposition towards learning that seeks deeper understanding then we get to spark one. I learn from the children I work with everyday, just as I learn from colleagues and researchers in Mind, Brain, and Education.

There is no one correct way to be a teacher; no universal system that works well for all students and all teachers. I don't believe that such a thing exists. However, people with vastly different experiences and perspectives can come together around shared values and the guiding lights that interdisciplinary research can provide. There will always be diversity within teaching just as there is diversity among people, and there will always be room for improvement and greater understanding.

All teachers bring *themselves* into the profession. We cannot help but bring our beliefs, values, and personal biographies into our teaching. So, let me share a little bit of mine. For over two decades, I have been a teacher, presenter, consultant, and teacher trainer. I have always viewed myself as an educator as well as a researcher. I officially began working for The Center for Transformative Teaching and Learning in 2015 to collaborate on the design of Mind, Brain, and Education (MBE) professional development for teachers and school leaders, but my own research predates that work. In 2011 I received a grant which allowed me to begin working on brain development and cognition in the ages I was teaching at the time (4-5 years). Before that – after finishing my graduate degree from Stanford University School of Education – I had the good fortune of working at a laboratory school, Bing Nursery School on Stanford's campus. Perhaps, the energy and influence of working at a school dedicated to the advancement of understanding children, child development, and education through on-going research made an impression upon me. Perhaps, it was the position title of teacher/ researcher that I had during my early teaching years in Reggio-Emilia inspired schools. But even before my professional career in education and my undergraduate and graduate years of schooling, I was a person who asked questions, sought deeper understandings of the world and the people in it, and placed tremendous value on the roles that creativity and imagination play in our lives. I did not know that I would end up dedicating my adult life to early childhood education at the time, but looking back, I see it as a natural next step.

I am an educator who sees merit in both progressive and traditional approaches towards education. I believe in the theory of constructivism's explanation of how children build meaning and knowledge through experience (often associated with progressive education), but I am also an educator who knows the value of direct instruction (often associated with traditional education). I believe that as a teacher, it is important to also be a researcher, to ask questions, and be continuously iterative. I believe that it is important for children to ask questions and that there is a symbiotic relationship between my inquisitive nature and that of my students.

Education is suffused with values and that is true even when we aim to focus on data sets and scientific findings. Education is about making and creating choices. Knowing that people have different ideas about what education ought to be, I think it is important that I state my own, here, in the beginning. For me, education aims to empower students with knowledge, skills, and the ability to think and act flexibly. This helps students develop an understanding of the world and themselves in it, so that they can live fulfilling lives as citizens of the world. This conception of education is linked to democracy; embedded in this idea is that of the value of an informed citizenry that thinks for themselves.

The terms 'education' and 'learning' might need clarification and teasing apart. We are all continuously learning in formal and informal, implicit and explicit, compulsory and voluntary ways throughout our lives, and this does not just happen in institutions of learning. *Learning* is a process of acquiring knowledge and skills. *Education* is an organized program for learning. Children come to us having already learned a lot about their world, and they will continue to learn outside of anyone's plans, lessons, curricula, and a school's scope and sequence. And just as they come to us with different background knowledge and unique biographies, they also come to us with unique dispositions *towards* learning. Those dispositions towards learning matter and so does how we help to form or dismantle them (see chapter one and throughout this book). In school, especially in those first years of schooling, children start to create a framework about what school is, what school offers *them*, how school helps them make sense of their world, and of course, how others play a role in that learning. These are important and powerful years.

Key Questions

As We Begin is informed by and focuses on the value of inquiry, intellectual curiosity, and creativity for both the teacher/learner and the student/

learner. This book seeks to contextualize MBE concepts in real early childhood classrooms, something that is currently lacking in the plethora of books and articles pertaining to MBE. In this book, you may find some things that create dissonance with your current practice or thinking and that might require some questioning, investigating, and research of your own. In this book I aim to hold the truths we know as classroom teachers alongside the truths of the science of teaching and learning.

Some of the guiding questions, compelling research findings, and insights in this book are my own, others I have collected from educators and theorists such as the inspirational and profound work of art education visionary, Elliott Eisner, and Loris Malaguzzi who founded the Reggio Emilia Approach. I also cite many studies with promising findings, most of which come from robust research in the field of Mind, Brain, and Education. As is the nature of science, research evolves, and educational implications and strategies often change along with it. In this ever-changing world of research, the need to keep curious and abreast of the ideas and findings out there never ceases. It is in this spirit that I hope the reader approaches the research and ideas laid forth.

Asking thoughtful questions matters, for they guide our work. The answers provide the opportunity to reorganize schemata, recalibrate, reconnect, and then come up with new questions. Questions invigorate, they open up new ways of seeing and thinking, and spark conversations with others. They give us something to strive for. I am concerned for children who do not have any questions just as I am concerned about educators who do not have questions. So, let us stay curious and continue to question. Some of the questions posed in this book are reflective and specific to *you*, the reader. What are *your* beliefs and values about early childhood and early childhood education? Is your practice aligned with those beliefs and values? Often a teacher holds certain beliefs, but feels compelled, for one reason or another, to use pedagogy that is counter to those beliefs. Awareness of this incongruence allows us to make necessary changes to our practice. Other recurring questions are: What do the various disciplines related to the mind, brain, learning, and early childhood say about a particular topic? Does my practice align with the research? What is the impact my practice is having on my students in both the short and long term?

I hope this book both validates and challenges you as a reader. I hope that it helps you make connections that clarify your own passions and motivations in this work. I hope that it creates an opportunity for you to build new schemata and bring that to bear in your practice. I hope that it sparks conversations with others. I hope this book reaffirms for you the importance of this work and inspires you to ponder, to wonder, and keep learning and growing in this field of early childhood education.

The structure of this book

This book is divided into three parts: Big ideas; Foundational Knowledge; and Zooming In. Similarly, each chapter is divided into three sections: the what; the why; and the how. *What* covers the knowledge. *Why* covers the underpinning reasons why this knowledge is important and impactful. *How* covers the suggestions that will help the educator align that research to their everyday practice.

As We Begin addresses big ideas and asks big questions of the field and the reader. It holds many complex ideas, theories, and areas of research. It invites reflection and conversation. It should not be read in one sitting. This is a book to read, digest, and then step away. Sit with the ideas and make connections to your practice, experience, and knowledge before continuing.

CHAPTER 1:
DISPOSITIONS OF MIND

The important outcomes of schooling include not only the acquisition of new conceptual tools, refined sensibilities, a developed imagination, and new routines and techniques, but also new attitudes and dispositions. The disposition to continue to learn through-out life is perhaps one of the most important contributions that schools can make to an individual's development. This achievement of mind rooted in motivational and dispositional factors is the source of continued transformation.

Elliott Eisner (2002)

Prevailing moods, outlooks, and tendencies can be cultivated over time. This book uses the term 'dispositions of mind' – that is, the thoughts and feelings we have about thinking and learning – to address how we can nurture learning, thinking, creating, and connecting with others. In bringing together research on brain development in early childhood, concepts from Mind, Brain, and Education (MBE), and theories about education, I will return time and again to dispositions of mind, in both learners and teachers.

Nature and nurture both play roles in how our brains develop, our dispositions of mind, and who we are. While all human brains are unique, they also have many reliable and generalizable similarities in development, structure, and function. Humans have exceedingly complex brains and all of the large fiber bundles are already present at birth. Babies come prewired for knowledge of objects, numbers, probabilities, space, and people (Deheane, 2020). We could categorize these facts as 'nature', but that is really just the beginning.

Neuroplasticity, a foundational MBE truth, refers to the ability of our brain to rewire throughout our lives due to need and circumstances (such as our experiences), environments, and relationships. As child and adolescent psychiatrist and founder of Turnaround for Children, Pamela Cantor, has said our brains and our genes are really a collaboration between nature and nurture. There is no separation between the two because 'genes are chemical followers'; gene expression is context dependent. As Fischer and Bidell (2006) express it, 'There is no separation of nature and nurture, biology and environment, or brain and behavior, but only a collaborative coordination between them'. This is why Mind, Brain, and Education (MBE) is an integration of fields related to Mind (psychology, cognitive psychology, and sociology), Brain (biology, neuroscience, and educational neuroscience), and Education (pedagogy and didactics) – or to put it another way, both nature and nurture.

In the context of development and learning, positive experiences and relationships of trust help to shape beneficial dispositions of mind that propel our motivations, growth, and happiness. Likewise, cognition and emotion are inherently linked (see chapter eight). In essence, these dispositions of mind are developed and fostered through experiences, moments of discovery, relationships with peers and teachers, and the feelings a child has about their own learning and place in the world. Teachers play a big role in a learner's developing disposition of mind.

Students

Educators and parents want their children to engage in intellectual and emotion-rich endeavors. We want children to be intrigued by ideas that propel them to examine and explore. We want them to wonder, reflect, be curious, and consider implications for themselves and the world. We want them to ponder their role in the world or in another person's life, to seek knowledge from others whose experience is different from from their own, to think deeply and actively search for connections and meaning. This is what it means to have a disposition of active inquiry for the purpose of meaning-making, understanding, and connection.

The learner with this disposition of mind is self-directed and inspired to tackle intellectual challenges, set goals, monitor progress, and connect with others.

Learners with this disposition often also have a drive to imagine and conjure up original mental imagery, to make unique connections, and to use different forms of representation to express a feeling or another way of conceiving. Curiosity and creativity often go together, and these are powerful human drives. This is how we, as humans, broaden and deepen knowledge, create, innovate, imagine better outcomes, collaborate, and seek peace and understanding. As the work of the affective neuroscientist Mary Helen Immoridino-Yang illustrates in her studies, this type of thinking is correlated with brain growth, better self-identity coherence, healthier relationships, and happier adults living fulfilling lives (Gotlieb & Immordino-Yang, 2023).

We often talk about what we want children *to know* and be able *to do*, and these are the drivers of curriculum. But what about how we want children *to feel*? Do we not want children to feel inspired, intrigued, capable, and passionate about learning? Tracey Tokuhama-Espinosa has said that memory and attention are the two non-negotiable ingredients for learning, and that without them, learning cannot happen in the brain. Well, feelings are the gateway to memory and attention. Put another way, the feelings we experience – how our limbic system tags the sensory information – determines what we pay attention to, what we do not pay attention to, and *how much* as well as if we remember it. Emotions are central to attention and memory. This is why disposition of mind is profoundly relevant to education.

As Immordino-Yang (2016) describes:

> Emotions are not just messy toddlers in a china shop, running around breaking and obscuring delicate cognitive glassware. Instead, they are more like the shelves underlying the glassware; without them cognition has less support.

What really matters in terms of attaining a fulfilling life of learning is not what you know and what you can do, but your dispositions for thinking. How does it feel to think? Do you value learning? Do you try to understand and construct deeper meaning?

As we know, children are not going to instantly fall in love with the feeling of thinking deeply and learning just because we want them to. While children do have a proclivity towards being enthusiastically curious about phenomena, that curiosity and drive to learn does not necessarily sustain itself, nor does it carry over to all school subjects without help and encouragement from teachers and caretakers. Children need to feel safe and that they have purpose in their learning. They need to feel that their questions and voice are important, relevant to others, and valuable. As Cantor, et al (2021), put it:

> Belief in one's ability to grow, learn, and succeed through education – both in and out of the classroom – may be more important than any specific curriculum for predicting and nurturing educational outcomes and life successes.

If the true end goal is to help young children embark upon a path that leads to health, happiness, a sense of purpose, and a thirst for greater knowledge and understanding then we need to think seriously about what keeps us motivated and engaged with this world as learners and social beings. As educators, we think a lot about content (and content is important). However, the drive to sustain effortful learning and to think deeply and creatively, depends upon developing skills and dispositions that support engagement *with* and learning *about* the world. These in turn depend on the ways in which educators think intentionally about learning environments and relationships.

Teachers

Teachers are humans too. I know how simple and ridiculous that statement seems, but we (as a society) do, in fact, benefit from this reminder. All of the things that we know to be true for student learners are also true for teacher learners. As humans, our dispositions of mind not only affect our students, they also affect *our own* self-identity coherence, *our* drive to keep learning and growing, *our* relationships with others, and *our* happiness in the world.

We want the same disposition of mind for the teacher as we do for the child learner. Such a disposition sets a teacher up to be more engaged and attuned to their students and their learning potential. In essence, it sets them up to do their job more effectively, while being inspired and motivated to keep going. To design a curriculum and pedagogical approach that optimizes the conditions for learning and discovery, we have to know how the brain works. That is, we have to know how we as humans think, what motivates us, what holds our attention and, conversely, what inhibits us. This is not only true in a general sense, but also in how these ideas relate to the individual learner.

To inspire children and our colleagues (which I think is equally important), we have to strive to know them as people and make effortful attempts to know how to elicit the right emotions and provide the right opportunities for growth. That is a lot to know and do and the work is never done! That is why a disposition of mind that orients us to a continuous endeavor, striving for more understanding, and a commitment to deepen our knowledge as well as our impact is not only beneficial, but necessary.

I have met many teachers who have cultivated this disposition of mind themselves and that is why they do what they do. They aim to understand the world they live in as well as understand others and how to help them. They know that humans can strive towards continuous learning and improvement. They are curious and find the act of both teaching and learning to be thrilling and tremendously rewarding, despite its challenges. Further, most early childhood educators know there is something powerful happening in brain development and learning in their students, even if they are not familiar with the research. They know that the seeds that are planted at the beginning of a student's educational career make a difference later on. Many early childhood educators think carefully about the intellectual endeavors and inner thoughts of the children they teach.

I cannot help but reflect upon lessons from the distinctive educational approach developed in the postwar schools of the city of Reggio Emilia, Italy. Many international schools, including in the US, have been inspired by 'The Reggio Emilia' approach (some more successfully than others). It has also been studied extensively by researchers from American Universities including George Forman, Louise Cadwell, and Harvard's Project Zero, to name just a few. These Reggio Emilia-inspired schools – in their varying degrees – cultivate a disposition towards teaching that perpetuates inquiry and innovation.

The Reggio Emilia approach holds that:

- Children are protagonists, that actively and capably construct meaning.
- Children are collaborators, contributing to learning communities.
- Children are communicators, transmitting meaning in myriad forms.
- The environment is the third teacher, and space can be optimized for learning and relationships.
- Teachers are partners.
- Teachers are researchers (engaged in continuous discussion, interpretation, and iteration of their work).
- Documentation is key (making learning visible to teachers and learners).
- Parents are essential partners in the child's educational experience.

Ann Lewin-Benham, one of the first American educators to become interested in the Reggio schools and founder of Model Early Learning Center in Washington, DC, states that the 'best' practice in this approach is actually a cluster of practices 'that teachers do to prepare interest-laden environments, to help children become self-regulated, and to foster the drive to learn that is a human's birthright' (2011). This approach requires the teachers to think in a detailed, systematic, but flexible way to create learning experiences that promote children's inquiry and understanding. Implementing this approach is demanding. 'There is a myth of spontaneity surrounding the Reggio Approach that doesn't respect the deep intentionality of teaching and learning' (Jennifer Azzariti, 2022). What appears as spontaneity is actually a highly intellectual, intentional, and creative responsiveness, that is able to identify and exploit teachable moments as they emerge from the children's interests and comments. This type of teacher response is only made possible by the knowledge, intention, and experience of the teacher.

Forgive the cliche, but teaching is both a science and an art. There is a science to learning and teaching that is continuously evolving, being understood, and applied in schools and classrooms. And there is an art to teaching. A teacher, like an artist, finds their own voice while creating environments, cultures, and opportunities. They consider school lessons, relationships, and how to evoke emotions to compel, inspire, puzzle, and motivate. A good friend and colleague, Peter Merrill, once said that 'master teachers are more like jazz musicians than symphony orchestra conductors'. Both the conductor and jazz musician manage many moving parts and require technical knowledge, skill, as well as vision to bring people together to create harmony. However, jazz musicians are also able to respond to what is happening in the moment, to shine a light on each individual musician, and to improvise collectively in the creative process. This is a useful metaphor for the disposition of mind of the teacher. When we see the work that we do as being simultaneously a science and an art, we are driven to be both knowledgeable and creative in our professional growth.

The interplay of teachers and students

Even the youngest children develop an awareness of their teacher's emotions, enthusiasm for teaching, and intentions. Toddlers and older children alike evaluate adult actions and perceived mental states and distinguish between intentional and unintentional actions (Dunfield & Kuhlmeir, 2010; Vaish, Carpenter, & Tomasello, 2010; Woo & Spelke, 2023). This is an area which cognitive developmental psychologists have been studying for some time. 'Children's own action planning, and their reasoning about their own mental states, develop hand in hand with their understanding of the actions and mental states of others' (Spelke & Shutts, 2020; Comallie, et al, 2016). This is significant to early childhood education because a) these cognitive developments are critical foundations for school readiness and b) these 'others' include the teachers. Before children can learn from teachers, they need a basic understanding of what the role of teacher is, how they feel about this role, and their teachers' intentions of trying to impart knowledge, skills, and the joy of learning. This helps children to make connections between their own intentions and actions at school.

Studies have been done on the so-called chameleon effect, whereby we unintentionally match our behavior to those around us. As John Hattie and Klaus Zierer state, 'Teachers can serve as role models by being passionate, and by bringing our competence and mindframes to bear we can get our students to adopt similar mindframes' (2018). In a longitudinal study in middle school math classrooms Frenzel, et al (2009) demonstrated that teacher enthusiasm and enjoyment of learning while teaching is positively linked to student enjoyment. A follow up study found that this is in fact a reciprocal relationship in which the enthusiasm of the students also transmits and affects the enjoyment of the teacher. Enjoyment of learning has also been correlated with promoting resilience, laying the groundwork for individual self-regulation, and guiding positive group behavior (Fredrickson, 2001). The teacher's disposition of mind is not only important to their own professional growth but impacts the disposition of mind of their students and therefore, the learning and growing that occurs in their classroom.

I would like to suggest a parallel between the impact of a teacher's enthusiasm and enjoyment, and of a teacher's adoption of a disposition of mind that seeks to actively question, make new connections, and understand their world and their role in it. It stands to reason that a teacher who is constantly seeking to better understand their craft – the science and art of teaching and learning – will also have a positive effect on their students. This is the result of not only understanding and engaging with their students better, but also of modeling intellectual curiosity, caring, persistence, and the value of actively seeking deeper understanding.

Pedagogy

We can think of our role in fostering dispositions of mind in three ways: pedagogy, curriculum, and environment. Pedagogy refers to the approaches and techniques through which the educator facilitates learning and includes the important relationship-building aspect of that work. Beyond creating a classroom culture that is supportive and responsive to the needs of the children, the early childhood educator has a lot to consider: play, literacy, numeracy, social cognition, communication, intellectual curiosity, creativity, imagination, and care.

Curriculum

The other way we influence learning and dispositions of mind is through curriculum. Curriculum refers to content and its organization. Curricular decisions are decisions about what aspects of the world of knowledge and the world of skills are worth focusing on. Naturally, pedagogy and curriculum overlap with elements of the designed environment which is the third category that contributes to learning and the dispositions of mind towards learning.

Environment

In the initial days and weeks of the school year, teachers put a lot of thought and effort into establishing a classroom culture. The physical environment plays a large part in this process in both implicit and explicit ways. The physical spaces we create, the artwork on display, the way learning is made visible, the materials available, and the care we take to keep the classroom organized and inviting are statements we are making to the children. Children don't just walk into a physical environment when they enter a classroom, it is an environment of routines, expectations, and relationships. Is it a welcoming environment? Is it an environment that encourages inquiry, risk-taking, collaboration, and creativity? Both these physical and perceived environments contribute to the overall *culture* of a classroom. The word 'culture' has many definitions and meanings. In the biological sciences (drawing on its Latin root, *cultivare*, to grow or till), culture is a medium for growing things. In the anthropological sense, culture is a shared way of life. In early childhood classrooms, teachers are helping to create a culture that supports growth *and* a shared way of growing and learning together.

Summary

Disposition of mind is the key concept in this book. It is the big idea that connects all of the other big ideas. Certain dispositions nurture learning, thinking, creating, and connecting with others and this is what we want for both students *and* teachers. A disposition of mind oriented towards active inquiry and making connections between ideas and people is connected to well-being. This is true when children are young and is also true as they grow up and find their role in the world. Curiosity and creativity often go together, and these drives are powerful. They are how we broaden and deepen our knowledge, create and innovate, imagine better outcomes, collaborate with others, and seek peace and understanding.

How classrooms and schools are organized is important and influences the development of a disposition of mind towards learning in students. The relationships that exist between the teachers and students (and each other), what is taught explicitly and implicitly, the norms and values that are embraced by the school culture, and the feelings made possible in these rooms and buildings will shape the associations that children will develop and carry for years to come about the roles of teachers, peers, and themselves as learners. These experiences, become part of a child's narrative about what school is and what learning can offer them. In these early years of schooling a child's perception of themselves, their own identity, and how they see themselves as part of a learning community is forming. For children to engage positively with learning in school (and beyond) it is critical that they develop positive perceptions as early as possible. Unfortunately, we all know how ubiquitous it is for children to develop persistent negative perceptions. Disposition of mind is something to make central to our thinking as educators for it is central to our students (and our own) growth.

Yet, as educators (and some of us, as parents), we are interested in more than just how a disposition of mind contributes to success in school. We are interested in students' ability to use what they have learned in school to enrich their lives *outside* and *beyond* school. Fostering the disposition to continue to learn throughout life might be one of the most important goals we have as educators.

Invitation to inquiry

- In three words or short phrases, how would you describe your own disposition of mind towards learning?
- Likewise, how would you describe your disposition of mind towards teaching?
- Can you think of specific students or children you have known that embody a positive disposition of mind towards learning? What is it about the way they engage with others, the world, and learning that leads you to believe this?

- Can you think of specific students or children you have known that do not exude a love of learning or intrinsic motivation to inquire and explore? If so, what does that look like?

- Accepting the belief that all children are curious, creative, and capable, how can we tap into their interests when these are not overtly shared?

- Some children do exude a positive disposition of mind towards learning, but present reticence or a lack of trust when it comes to learning in school. Can you think of specific students or children you have known that would fit this description? If so, what does that look like?

- Can you think of a time in which you, as an educator, felt particularly passionate and alive during a lesson, project, or line of inquiry? Did you observe this affecting the students you were working with? What were those times, and did they have lasting effects?

CHAPTER 2:
THE TEACHER/RESEARCHER

Research is formalized curiosity. It is poking and prying with a purpose.

Zora Neal Hurston (quoted in Kaplan, 2003)

Elaborate apparatus plays an important part in the sciences of today, but I sometimes wonder if we are not inclined to forget that the most important instrument in research must always be the mind ...

W. I. B. Beveridge (1957)

When teachers make listening and documentation central to their practice, they transform themselves into researchers.

Carlina Rinaldi (2012)

Bloom famously stated in his 1984 '2 Sigma' paper that 'what one child can do, nearly all children can do under highly favorable conditions.' Simple, yet profound, this statement can inspire but also intimidate teachers as they grapple with their mission as an individual teacher. A teacher might ask themselves: what are these highly favorable conditions and what can I do to help create them? How much power do I really have to positively impact the learning trajectory of my students? What are the conditions that foster the development of productive and engaged learners that acquire complex and adaptive skills? How are these conditions affected by background or other challenges? These are big questions. Regardless of the student's developmental or circumstantial starting point, teachers want to drive growth and the children's belief in their own ability to learn and develop. In this chapter I will suggest that one way to do this is through the approach of the 'teacher/researcher'.

I define a 'teacher/researcher' as a practitioner who continuously seeks new knowledge and understanding and uses it as the basis to alter their approach and improve outcomes. To do this, the teacher/researcher must have a way to measure or assess impact. The teacher/researcher is a student themself, not just in the field of education (and contributing fields), but of their individual students. This concept of a teacher/researcher is connected to that of disposition of mind explored in the previous chapter. Teacher/researchers want to know *how* to set our students along positive learning trajectories that allow the fullest expression of their developmental range while instilling within them a sense of their own self-efficacy. They want students to be intrinsically motivated to deepen or elevate their current understandings as well as to learn something entirely new, and to have a disposition of mind that approaches learning with excitement.

One of the many benefits of teaching a young age group is that the spirit of lively and active research is likely in the room already. In other words, there are already many little 'researchers' in the classroom, and hopefully, adult-sized ones as well. As we know, young children, like young researchers, are always collecting information, whether it be objects, pictures, experiences, observations, or ideas. The way children pursue their own ideas, how they play, make up stories, make connections and engage in questioning is all part of their 'research'.

By paying close attention, making our own observations, creating experiences and iterations, and pursuing our own ideas about what is happening in the minds of children both cognitively and emotionally, we as teachers learn about our students as individuals. However, we are also gathering useful data about the process of learning itself. Learning begets learning begets learning in both the students and the teachers. In my early childhood classrooms I often teach the concept of positive reciprocating loops. This is a great example of one.

All teachers use, interpret, and create knowledge

I think many would readily acknowledge that teachers both use knowledge (of content, pedagogy, research, the individual learner, etc.) and interpret knowledge (of theory, research, behavior, learning outcomes, etc.). But we are also *knowledge creators*. By making creative connections between disparate sources of information to address the individual and their learning, we are bringing new knowledge into the world. We do this both as we plan and in the moment. Everything we know from practice, theory, and research comes together and is applied when we are in the act of teaching.

As Newkirk puts it, background knowledge informs our decisions, but the problem-solving and 'theorizing that is more immediate for teachers is much more localized, provisional, and fine-grained. It is often day-specific, group-specific, child-specific, task-specific, weather-specific, and even self-specific' (2015). Put simply, in the classroom, we are informed by general truths, theories of learning, and research, but we are also dealing with highly specific situations and individuals. It is this responsiveness – this thinking on our feet and constant evaluation of the emotional states, cognitive load upon, and engagement of the students – that informs the decisions and adjustments that characterize great teaching.

Teaching is a creative act. Similarly, when we engage with different learning experiences to capitalize on an interest or momentum in the classroom, we are *creating knowledge*. These creations are all examples of 'teacher research'. However, these creations are not always shared with others in our building let alone in the wider field.

Why is this delineation of teacher knowledge useful?

It is imperative that teachers are seen as knowledge creators if we are going to contribute to the field of MBE and have dialogue with those in academia. Although not all teachers want to be in dialogue with researchers and policy makers, teachers' input is needed in MBE to help develop more precise theories and strategies for effective and practical pedagogy and curricula. When it comes to making decisions and seeking and creating usable knowledge for the benefit of the students, both academic research and teachers' local knowledge of their students and classrooms have a place.

Research from academia

Educational theory provides many broad explanations and generalizations that have great practical utility. Academic research offers the teacher tested ideas, strategies, explanations, and lines of inquiry. As is the nature of science, research evolves, and theories and strategies can change over time. As teacher/researchers look to research from academia, it is important that they keep in mind some caveats. Some studies show promise but are not yet fully supported by robust research or meta-analysis. Recommendations can change. There is no one strategy that works for all students, all the time. Following research developments in the field of MBE is an ongoing process rather than a 'one and done' event. When looking to research to inform their practice, teacher/researchers should always keep in mind the particulars of their students, their context, and their own professional experience and knowledge.

As teachers, we want to be informed by academic research and pay attention to its claims about predictability, but we also want to see how it applies in our own classroom and with our students. We want academic research to *inform* our practice, not *decide* what we do for us. You don't just land on a theory and accept it uncritically, you must stay observant and explore whether in application the theory still holds or not, whether it is helping your students or not.

Academic research has the potential to elevate and empower our pedagogy. Absorbing new knowledge enriches the interpretations and decisions we make daily in the classroom making them more flexible and complex. As Stanislas Dehaene states, 'I am deeply convinced that one cannot properly teach without possessing, implicitly or explicitly, a mental model of what is going on in the minds of the learners' (2020). Mind, Brain, and Education research can guide our teaching by grounding our understanding of the minds of learners in science. However, every brain (and person) is different and research from academia cannot predict exactly how a concept or methodology will look in a particular classroom, or with a particular teacher, or learner. The work that teachers do as active learners, with the ballast of their experience, and relationship-building with students, is in turn crucial to our collective knowledge and expertise in the wider field of education.

Research in the classroom

Knowledge building in science is necessarily a slow and meticulous process. It proceeds brick by brick as studies are conceived, funded, created, performed, interpreted, written, and reviewed. This gradual laying of bricks continues as scientists consider earlier findings, make iterations, consider limitations, methods, causation, and inference. Teaching, on the other hand, happens in real time. Teachers receive data all the time every day and oftentimes teachers make decisions to alter or modify a lesson plan in the moment. This is one ubiquitous way that data collection, albeit informally gathered, influences decisions a teacher makes and the path a class may take.

Teachers can intentionally and carefully design curricula and activities for the purpose of addressing a challenge. They can also do so for the purpose of creating an opportunity. If a teacher is engaged in a cycle of observing, analyzing, strategizing, and measuring impact in their classroom (and many already are), then that teacher is already a teacher/researcher. The level of formality that we bring to classroom research will depend on different factors. A teacher might have a particular goal in mind and try ideas out without creating a graphic organizer for collecting data and measuring impact. That teacher is still engaged in teacher research. A more formalized approach, however, would include a method that allows for the recording (and possible sharing) of observation, analysis, strategies, and impact.

What would a more formalized approach look like? For example, a teacher might want to focus on reflective learning (metacognition), or collaboration in group projects. In either of these two cases, a particular question or goal (metacognition or collaboration) leads the teacher to design strategies and then measure their impact. Then the strategies are applied, data is collected, and the resulting findings and ideas are shared and analyzed with colleagues. Subsequently, iterations can be made, and the process continues.

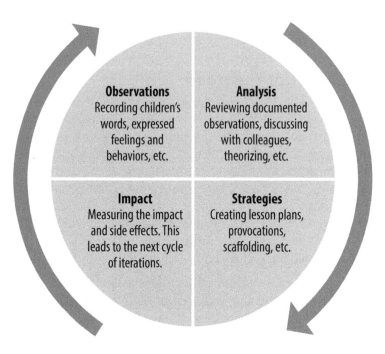

Creating a graphic organizer to order your observations, analysis, strategies, and results can be a great first step to increasing your understanding of and impact in your classroom. Having a system for sharing and discussing such documentation with colleagues can also have a multiplier effect.

Glenn Whitman and Ian Kelleher lay out similar ways of performing classroom research in their book, *Neuroteach: Brain science and the future of education.* Beginning with an idea or interest, the teacher reads peer-reviewed research in the field of Mind, Brain, and Education and then 'translates' ideas or questions from that research into their own classroom context. They then create a research plan or protocol, record data, and measure impact; this process then shapes subsequent decisions about strategies and goals for learning in the classroom. Alternatively, the project begins with a novel concept/approach/strategy that is proposed to increase learning in the classroom. This might be supported by academic literature (but not necessarily). However, the proposed approach should be grounded in a solid understanding of how brains learn and develop. Then – as with the previous approach – a plan is designed that includes the explicit laying out of a goal or goals, and protocols for measuring and recording impact, sharing ideas and theories with colleagues, and making iterations.

After a research plan has been carried out, there are many ways teachers can share their work with other teachers and scholars; these include in-house meetings and collaborations, presentations at conferences, journal articles, online media, etc. In the end, however, what matters most is not how the research is shared, but that the teacher's practice and the learning experiences in their classroom are transformed by the process. If the teacher becomes intrigued, inspired, and/or motivated to follow an idea or line of questioning that could lead to better outcomes for their students, change and reflection will likely follow in a reciprocating loop.

This is the disposition of mind of the teacher/researcher – one of continually finding ways to improve their craft, through knowledge seeking and building, data collection, reflection, and iteration. This kind of work is inspiring and motivational to not only the teacher/researcher but to others in the field, be they colleagues, or even students.

Three main categories for classroom research

There are three main categories of classroom research: **pedagogy**, **curriculum**, and **environment**. Pedagogy includes strategies for engagement, attention, memory, assessment, emotion, motivation, lesson design, and teacher-student relationships. Curriculum covers content, concepts, interdisciplinary approaches, and the organization and the structure of content. Environment refers to student well-being, belonging, classroom culture, the influence of available materials, access to outdoor learning, learning beyond the classroom walls, and the physical design of space. Naturally, these three areas overlap greatly. To advance the learning of both the teacher and the student, attention to professional development needs to be balanced with research into all of these areas.

Below is list (non-exhaustive) of possible areas for research in early childhood education:

	Feedback (necessarily highlighting non-discursive forms).
	Metacognitive skills and metacognitive knowledge.
	Formative assessment to inform pedagogy and curriculum.
	Play as a means to increase student engagement and understanding.
	Belonging and student engagement.
	Ways of fostering intrinsic motivation and intellectual curiosity.
	Designing classroom environment and access to materials to elicit inquiry, deeper engagement, or specific learning needs.
	Teaching social cognitive skills.
	Incorporating the visual and performing arts to increase student access, understanding, expression, and engagement.
	Practicing and developing executive function skills.

Support fellow teacher/researchers

Collaboration can have a powerful positive impact on the teacher/ researcher. It not only keeps those questions and ideas flowing, but the sense of partnership, that we have allies, can keep us going in what can feel like difficult though meaningful work. It can be tremendously helpful if your school has a culture that supports collaboration between colleagues explicitly, for example by making time in the school calendar for research collaborations.

When looking to support a colleague in their research, or develop a collaboration around that research, a framework like one below may be useful to identify areas in which you can contribute.

Practice or Strategy Used	
Educator's Name	
Class or Age Group	
What was the goal or opportunity the educator was trying to attain or create?	
What impact did or does this practice or strategy appear to have on the child/ children?	
What are iterations or modifications that could make it better?	
How can I be an ally in this work for the benefit of the students?	
How can I be an ally to this work for the benefit of our collective knowledge and growth?	
How can I be an ally to this individual educator?	

There are many reasons why this type of collegial collaboration and support can be hard but let's just name a few. Firstly, this level of collaboration requires relationship-building. Time, attention, and effort need to be devoted to developing and sustaining a good working relationship. The payoff is that this type of relationship will allow trust and therefore personal growth to occur. Secondly, excessive competition between teachers can squash opportunities for growth. Some of you reading this will know exactly what I am referring to while others may be surprised by this idea. A healthy level of competition in all fields is good because it can be a motivator to keep people at 'the top of their game'. However, when the level of competition between colleagues is too great, trust is lost or never established. This environment is not a safe space for collaboration. Teachers working in this environment will not contribute ideas or try new things for fear of consequences such destructive criticism or a lack of support. In this situation, many ideas that have the potential to have a positive impact will never be explored and teacher creativity and motivation will be stifled. A third reason why true collaboration is hard to achieve and maintain is the amount of time needed to make it work. Finding time in the work week to go beyond the myriad things that teachers already do, for research, reflection, discussion, iteration, etc. is hard. This ubiquitous time problem can make the goal of collaboration among teacher/researchers seem near impossible. However, when you consider the potential gains in student success in terms of well-being and achievement, teacher well-being and achievement, and school achievement and reputation, there is no question as to whether collaboration and research are worth the time or not.

Reggio Emilia teacher/researchers

A core belief among educators in Reggio Emilia schools is that teachers are researchers in the classroom. That is not to say that they all hold PhDs, run controlled experiments, and publish data in peer-reviewed journals. Rather, it means that their approach to teaching includes a serious commitment to the careful and documented observation of children and that instructional decisions are based upon these observations. The aim is to generate new ideas. Reggio Emilia teacher/researchers use rigorous examination of problems through multiple perspectives. The practice of teacher/research grows from the belief that the teacher's own learning should parallel that of the children they teach, and be characterized by a spirit of inquiry, purpose, and agency.

As researchers, teachers use an iterative process whereby they observe and listen to children; they then design experiences, prepare materials and provocations, theorize, observe, and document … before analyzing the children's words and actions, and once more reflecting and theorizing. The aim is learning, growth, and expression. In the process of thoughtfully documenting the children's learning processes – in visual ways which are accessible to the children – they are acknowledging the children, whom they also consider to be researchers. This approach can be described as a way of using rigorous examination towards a goal of innovation (Edwards & Gandini, 2015). Teacher/researchers are also part of a collaborative network with other teacher/researchers. While some aspects of the Reggio Emilia professional development structure have evolved over the years, the goal remains the same, which is to continuously elevate education through reflection, inquiry, and innovation. Research should be collaborative, explicit with its purpose, systematic, and transparent. It should not be top-down, but rather diffuse, creating and supporting collegial zones of knowledge creation and exchange.

The teacher/researcher and the mind of an expert

The difference between the mind of an expert and a novice is not just content they know, but its organization. Experts incorporate new information into a complex system of categories and subcategories. One can think of the metaphor of a filing cabinet; it sorts information, but also shows how the various files connect. As new information or a new schema is created, the expert can reorganize their existing schemata to make sense of it. On a physiological level (to be explored further in the following chapter on the brain), the expert has created denser and more efficient neural networks. They can then analyze new content in relation to its context. More content, better organization, and an understanding of context also means that experts can remember and learn more easily within their area of expertise. The novice, on the other hand, does not have any of this (yet).

As experts, veteran teachers have complex filing systems that they draw upon when planning: in developing curriculua, creating lessons, conducting parent-teacher conferences, and writing report cards. Expert teachers also draw upon these in their responsive, moment-to-moment decisions while considering the idiosyncrasies of the day, the material, and specific students. Sometimes the best plan is to abandon the plan and go in a new direction – this type of cognitive flexibility is also a hallmark of an expert. Dense and efficient neural networks allow the expert teacher to respond with intention and oftentimes, that means doing so on the spot and while balancing student emotions!

To be an expert, however, does not mean that one already knows everything there is to know about a subject, or that all of our ideas are great. Ideally, experts have the humility to let go of ideas that are not working and to accept good suggestions from other people. The humble expert understands the importance of having even more files or filing cabinets to elucidate their understanding and practice. The Dunning-

Kruger Effect (named after psychologists David Dunning and Justin Kruger) is a cognitive bias whereby people with limited knowledge in a particular domain tend to overestimate their own knowledge or competence. This is because a high level of current knowledge is needed to have the metacognitive ability to recognize our own deficiencies in that domain. Oftentimes, it can feel like the more we know, the less we know.

To conduct research of any kind, be it in the classroom, in the library, on the internet, or in the lab, it is first necessary be aware that there is something we do *not* know. That awareness is what pushes our knowledge and abilities as individuals, as a culture, and as a species. The founder of TED Conferences, Richard Saul Wurman, talks about one of his motivators being to understand something that he did not previously, not necessarily to change it, but simply to understand it. During an interview in 2014, he stated, 'My power and why I am more powerful than anybody in this room is that I embrace my ignorance more than you embrace your ignorance'. There is a forceful yet refreshing quality to that statement. We don't need to be afraid to admit ignorance! In fact, admitting ignorance will likely lead to growth. Often people treat the admittance of ignorance as abhorrent, never to be done aloud. Wurman flips this on its head. Awareness of what we do not know or fully understand is what keeps us searching for more and better understanding. The mind of the expert teacher knows that mastery is never fully attained, it broadens and lengthens, it informs and questions, it creates and re-creates, all in the process of establishing ever-more intricate and usable filing systems.

One last point about the mind of the expert and teacher/researchers: expert teachers have transferable skills. A transferable skill is one that can serve as a template for learning in a variety of domains and settings. Transferable skills are desirable as they can be applied to novel situations and allow for the generation of unique solutions. If teachers have acquired a skill set – for example, observation, reflection, and iteration in one domain – they might be able to apply or transfer that same set of skills to other domains. A transferable skill set like this opens doors and potentially leads to mindshifting endeavors.

The teacher/researcher, behavior, and classroom management

So far, we have spent a lot of time talking about the importance of the teacher/researcher's approach to teaching and learning. Now, I want to connect the concept more directly to student behavior. Most teacher preparation or mentoring programs include classroom management tips and strategies. Teachers are even evaluated on their classroom management skills. But what would a research-informed classroom management rubric look like? Is there such a thing? Could there be? To some classroom management is synonymous with classroom control. Although it doesn't have to be, classroom control is often associated with rules and children diligently abiding by them. Rules are necessary, especially when it comes to the physical and emotional safety of the children. And rules are especially effective when students have some agency in creating them. Rules help provide predictability and justice, and this benefits all. But if a child demonstrates a 'deviant' behavior and our response is to quickly enforce a rule, we might lose the opportunity to understand what is behind that behavior. The teacher/researcher wants to understand more before automatically reacting. If we teach in the spirit of listening and observing, with intention and inquiry, then we are more likely to notice complex and important aspects of individuals and their learning. We can hypothesize about the reason behind a behavior we notice, make informed decisions, and then reflect on and possibly alter our hypothesis as to the cause and our best response.

Let's look at an example from my mixed-age preschool classroom. It was late morning and we had various activities set up for children to choose from at 'centers' around the room. Each center was carefully planned and prepared and was designed to address a particular skill or learning experience. All of the centers were explained, and the children were told to pick a center at which to engage. One child chose to practice summersaults on the rug instead of one of the prepared centers. He had plenty of space and his movements were not creating an unsafe situation for him or others. I watched him with curiosity for a moment and documented his choice. My supervisor walked by and asked why I was letting him do this. I answered that I was letting him make this choice for multiple reasons:

- I was aware that this particular school does not have a PE class and does not provide a lot of outdoor recess time.
- I knew that this child – who has a lot of energy – needed to find ways of using it so that he could focus on other tasks.
- I knew that this was his way of self-regulating,
- He was learning something about the use of his gross motor skills to propel his body forward in a safe way; he was hypothesizing, experimenting, and iterating right in front of me.
- Most importantly, the child was making this choice because it was addressing a need he felt he had, and I wanted to observe first to understand what that need was. Then, I wanted to consider the best way to support him while also supporting the needs of the other children and our curricular goals.

Reflecting on this I had some further thoughts. Was there a way I could turn this into a more organized teaching moment? Could I have him record and graph his techniques? Should I suggest that he organize a small group and teach them how to do summersaults? If so, would I ask him to make a plan and consider the needed materials and the space needed (like a mat or a spread of flat grass)? Or would it be better to simply validate his need to move and use his muscles, but remind him that there is another time and space where he would be able to do this? Either way, as a teacher/researcher I feel like it is my job to take the moment necessary to understand the behavior, validate the child, and then offer possible alternatives or extensions. My supervisor did not realize I was going to give such a long answer!

Mental models of the brain

Brain anatomy and development, and knowledge of how information travels along neurons, is not part of the training or background of most teachers. At some point, many of us have wondered how our knowledge and training of 'best practices' aligns with actual brain development and brain change. However, not many of us have found the time to gain such knowledge, and there are many context dependent as well as systemic reasons for that. Nonetheless, having a mental model of the brain and the development of neural networks is a powerful and transformation thing.

It is the foundational knowledge for understanding concepts and theories from the science of learning. The next chapter will lay that foundation by exploring the anatomy, function, and structure of the brain.

Summary

A teacher/researcher is willing to continuously tweak and alter their approach as they gain understanding not just of the field, but of their students as individuals. Accordingly, teacher/researchers are knowledge users, interpreters, and creators. As knowledge creators, teachers have the potential to contribute greatly to their specific students' learning trajectories as well as the wider field of education, thus benefiting all teachers and learners. Teacher/researchers are motivated to stay abreast of research coming out of academia and finding ways to incorporate these ideas and strategies into their practice while attending to the needs of specific individual learners. Whether their research is formalized or casual, teacher/researchers are collecting data, analyzing, applying strategies, and measuring impact. The three main categories under which most classroom research topics fall are: pedagogy, curriculum, and the environment. As one endeavors to engage in classroom research, one cannot underestimate the value of a network of supportive colleagues. We can create systems to encourage this level of collaboration and feedback among peers thus elevating our practice, knowledge, and sense of purpose. As we further develop this approach to learning and teaching – what I like to call a disposition of mind towards learning and teaching – we further our expertise and ability to broaden and deepen our conceptual frameworks (schemata).

Invitation to inquiry

- This chapter explores different ways of being a teacher/researcher. Are there ways in which you identify with this title? Are there ways in which you would like to grow into this role?

- How can we create a culture of teacher/researchers that grow, support, and learn from one another? Do you anticipate obstacles in this endeavor at you school? Who would be your allies in this work?

Further reading

Glover, Matt and Ellin Oliver Keene (2015) *The Teacher You Want to Be: Essays about children, learning, and teaching.*

Hattie, John and Klaus Zierer (2018) *10 Mindframes for Visible Learning: Teaching for success.*

PART 2:
FOUNDATIONAL KNOWLEDGE
(OUR BUILDING BLOCKS)

CHAPTER 3:
THE BRAIN

There, in fold after fold of gelatinous tissue, are masses of cell nuclei, axons, and synapses, shuttling electrical signals this way and that in a riotous web of neural activity. Far from chaotic, those neurons work in clusters, yes, but also across clusters. And these clusters swing and even dance. They do so, moreover, in ways partially determined by genetic and epigenetic substrates, environmental influences (both present and past), and social interactions. This is a complex system if there ever was one. A veritable symphony.

Perry Zurn and Dani S. Bassett (2022)

I can't help it. It is not me. It is my brain. It is like alive or something.

Sheldon, age four

Having a mental model of the brain and its neurons helps us to understand what is happening inside our own heads as well as those of the people we engage with. This knowledge is particularly relevant for teachers who literally work to alter other people's brains on a daily basis, although many of us don't think of ourselves in these terms. Hopefully, by the end of this chapter (and this book), readers will begin to identify as 'brain changers' and even be empowered and excited about it.

This chapter is about the neuroanatomy basics; it is, however, less about adopting a new vocabulary than about acquiring the mental imagery to anchor your understanding of how information moves and connects.

This foundational knowledge will help to clarify how humans react or respond to stimuli in a general sense, and more specifically what happens when we (as teachers or students) are grasping new concepts and solidifying information in long-term memory. With an understanding of basic neuroanatomy, we are better able to grasp why we learn some material successfully but struggle with other content, and why we are sometimes confronted with stubborn obstacles in processing new information or recalling that which we have previously learned. This is a powerful tool for all teachers.

If our job as teachers is to create the conditions in which learning can happen, we need a wide array of knowledge and skill sets. No single set of conditions, strategy, or environment is ideal for everyone, however, good design by an informed and motivated teacher, improves the odds for every student.

There are some undeniable neuroanatomical truths that confront us in the classroom each day. As Glenn Whitman – coauthor of *Neuroteach* – puts it, 'all students come to school with their brains' and 'the brain is the organ for learning'. Furthermore, the brain has the ability to grow and change over time through experience and repetition – we refer to this as neuroplasticity. In the following sections, I condense the key concepts and terms of neuroanatomy to help the reader see and conceptualize the brain as an organ for learning and build a mental model for what is going on in the minds and brains of learners.

Basic neuroanatomy

Let's begin with a basic understanding of the most notorious brain cell, the *neuron*. We will then move on to the basics of the brain structures while highlighting the systems, networks, and regions most relevant to teachers. Finally, we will build upon these concepts with a section about the specific brain development of young children, ages of three to six.

Brain cells: neurons

It is still hard to get my brain around (no pun intended) the fact that if we laid out our neurons from end to end, our neuron chain would be over two million miles long! As the physicist Michio Kaku once said, the human brain is the most complicated object in the known universe. A basic understanding of the structure and function of the neuron is essential for understanding how cognition happens in the brain. A mature neuron looks much like a tree with extensive roots (the *dendrites*), a trunk (the *axon*), a cell body, and branches (*axon terminals*).

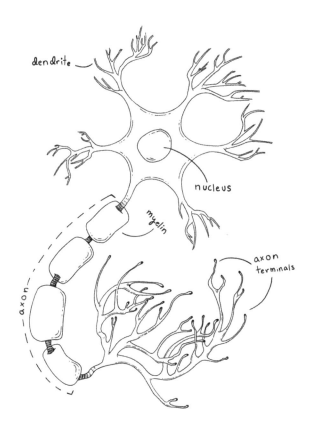

The dendrites receive information from other neurons and send it down the axon. They ultimately branch out to transfer information to the next neuron in the circuit from the axon terminals. The cell body containing the nucleus lies in between these two branch systems. Information is transmitted electrically within the neuron, but when it reaches the end of the axon branches or terminals it needs to cross a gap to reach the next neuron in the circuit. This gap is called the *synapse*.

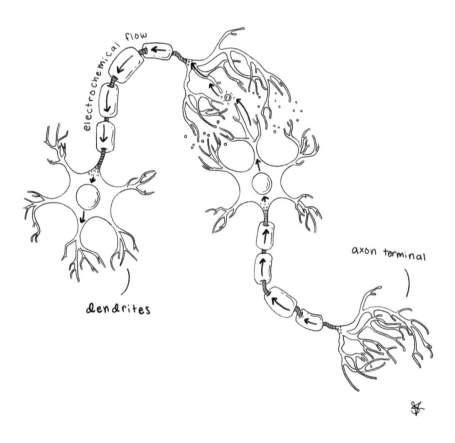

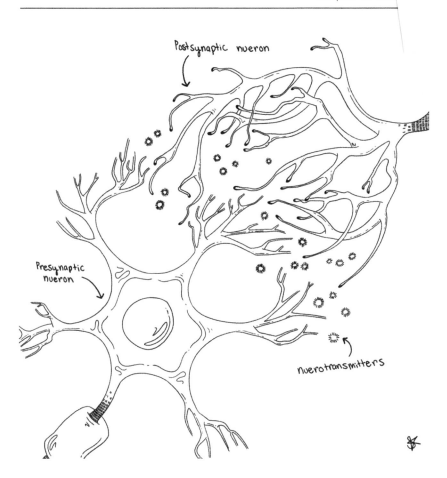

Information cannot cross the synapse electrically, rather it uses a chemical helper, the *neurotransmitter*. You can imagine the neurotransmitter like a little boat that crosses the synapse where they are met with special receptors on the postsynaptic neuron's dendrites. This then triggers an electrical response, and the journey goes on. This electrical and chemical transmission repeats itself through every cell and synapse of the circuit.

 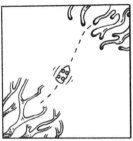 

One of the most powerful concepts that enhances our understanding of brain development and learning is Hebb's axiom (1949, 1955). It can be summarized by the mnemonic: *Neurons that fire together become wired together*. The consistent coaction of firing neurons leads to synaptic strength. Consistent firing and patterns of firing neurons produce more deeply ingrained neural pathways. With a mental model of what neurons look like, how information moves through and between them in an electro-chemical manner, and how neural connections build networks, this axiom not only makes sense, but elucidates a powerful concept in learning. Teachers can go back to this axiom again and again to help them understand various aspects of our craft. Rightly so, this axiom will come up explicitly (and implicitly) in this book several times.

A word about neurotransmitters

Neurotransmitters impact learning in a multitude of ways and that is why having a foundational understanding of what they are can be helpful. Neurotransmitters (i.e. the 'little boats') such as serotonin, tryptophan, norepinephrine, acetylcholine, and dopamine transport information across the synapses. They are released on one side of the synaptic gap and float to specialized receptors on the neighboring neuron. When learning is associated with joy or it satisfies a need to better understand something, dopamine is released thereby increasing focus and attention. According to Silvia Bunge, 'Dopamine is not released like other neurotransmitters in the synapses, but rather is sort of spritzed on large areas of the brain, which enhance the signaling of neurons' (quoted in Bronson & Merryman, 2010). Depleted neurotransmitters rebuild when we take a break and some neurotransmitters take longer than others.

Brain cells: Glial cells

There are two different types of cells in the nervous system: neurons (10%) and *glial* cells (90%). Glial cells can feel a little like the underdog when it comes to learning about the brain, but they are the support that provides the brain's structure and metabolic sustenance. Glial cells help the neurons correctly process information. There are different types of glial cells: in early development, one type of glial cell acts to extend long fibers that act as trails for neurons to follow. Other types of glial cells form *myelin* (more on this later). While yet others line blood vessels to control which chemical signals are permitted to pass into and out of the brain. Some glial cells have the function of forming the brain's defense system by removing foreign particles from dying cells. Neuroscientists continue to explore the role that glial cells play in brain function, and this is an area ripe for continued research and understanding.

Neurogenesis

As the term suggests, *neurogenesis* is the process of the formation of neurons and glial cells. The formation of the major brain structures begins early in pregnancy. Most neurons establish themselves during pregnancy and early infancy and will survive as long as the person lives, unlike the cells in other tissues of the body. These neurons migrate to their proper locations and begin wiring together in a process called synaptogenesis. It is currently believed that our neurons can collectively form up to 100 trillion connections. The growth of the connections (dendrites) between neurons is life-long. Neuroscientists continue to understand more about synaptic connections.

Pruning

During infancy and early childhood, the cerebral cortex has an overabundance of synapses, about twice as many as it needs. This makes for a lot of overlap and inefficiency. Over time, *neural pruning* makes for more precise and efficient transmission and storage of knowledge. Why does this happen? Some neuroscientists believe it is something akin to evolution and natural selection – that by over-producing synapses, the brain forces them to compete, allowing for the most useful synapses to take control. A very useful synapse is highly active. It receives more electrical impulses and releases greater amounts of neurotransmitters. 'Children lose on the order of 20 billion synapses per day between early childhood and adolescence' (Eliot, 1999). Don't worry! This process is necessary to streamline our mental processes. However, it is important to note that this may also explain why our processes become less flexible and perhaps, less creative as we grow older.

Myelination

Myelination is a critical event in neuronal development. Myelin is a fatty, white substance that coats the axons and acts as an insulator. It is not only essential for proper information flow but allows for greater speed in electrical transmission. 'Gray' brain matter refers to the branching dendrites of neurons and the synaptic connections they form while 'white' matter refers to the connecting neurons whose axons are covered in myelin.

Neurons and glia are organized in various levels of complexity. Small clusters of neurons are called *nuclei*. Larger assemblies are called *circuits*, *regions*, and *hemispheres*. Now, let's move onto the basic structure of the brain.

Basic structure of the brain

Now that we have a basic understanding of neurons and how they transmit information, let's look at the bigger picture. The brain is basically a collection of about 86 billion neurons; it is about 80% water, 10% fat, and 8% protein and weighs about 3 pounds. The development of the nervous system begins in utero and matures in a somewhat programmed sequence from the spinal cord up to the prefrontal cortex. Brain growth follows three general directions in a predictable way: from back to front, from inside out, and from the bottom up. A baby is born with almost fully developed lower-brain structures, the *spinal cord* and *brainstem*. After birth, other brain areas come into play such as the *cerebellum* and *basal ganglia* (both involved with movement), the *limbic system* (emotion and memory), and finally the *cerebral cortex* (willed behavior, rational thought, conscious experience), with the *prefrontal cortex* becoming fully developed as late as the early 20s for females and a little later in males. Sensory areas of the cerebral cortex develop relatively quickly followed by motor areas.

Scientists have divided the brain into lobes, and these are strongly associated with functions or behaviors. The *occipital lobe* is primarily responsible for vision (about 80-90% of all information most people absorb is visual). The *frontal lobe* is where higher-level thinking occurs, as well as purposeful acts and executive functions. The *parietal lobe* processes higher sensory and language functions, while the temporal lobes are associated with hearing, memory, meaning, and language. The *limbic system* takes up about 20% of brain volume and is located in the midbrain area (I will elaborate on the limbic system in the following section). However, there are also overlapping functions between brain lobes, and learning happens all over the brain, not in isolated regions. It is inaccurate to think that a certain type of thinking or behavior comes from *just* one region of the brain. In an fMRI, one actually sees brain activity patterns across multiple regions light up when the subject is given a task. In other words, while we may be talking about a structure that is most dominantly associated with a specific action or behavior, more often than not many other regions are involved as well.

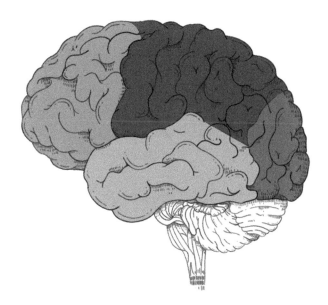

The limbic system (emotion and memory)

The limbic system is a large set of neural structures that helps to govern our emotions (amongst other functions). It sits right in the divide between the cerebral cortex and the brain stem. Two limbic system structures of particular relevance to early childhood educators are the *amygdala*, which is associated with emotion, and the *hippocampus*, which is associated with memory.

The amygdala gives us the raw manifestations of emotion such as fight or flight responses. Communication between our prefrontal cortex and our limbic system allows for awareness of our feelings and our ability to regulate them. Thus, while the limbic system expresses pure, instinctive emotion, the brain has the ability to regulate our responses according to the teaching, training, and experience of the individual.

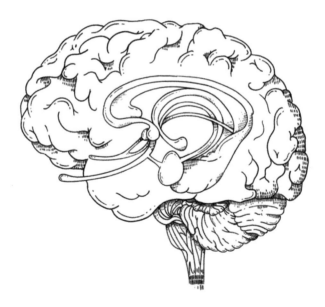

While the development of a healthy limbic system is crucial in a general sense, its relevance for early childhood education cannot be overstated. While it is common to keep careful track of every motor milestone and academic achievement of young children, the rapid development of their emotional abilities is sometimes overlooked. This aspect of brain development is 'in many ways the most important one of all, because it establishes the critical foundation on which every other mental skill can flourish' (Eliot, 1999). This will be elaborated upon further in chapter eight on emotion and cognition.

The neural networks necessary for mature emotional regulation take a long time to develop and this process continues into early adulthood. However, helping to establish these networks while children are young is crucial to their healthy development. 'The ability of the cortex to function optimally depends on the healthy formation of the limbic system beneath'(Stamm, 2007).

The amygdala

Within the limbic system lies a particularly important part of the brain known as the amygdala. The amygdala are two small, almond-shaped structures nestled between the cortex and the subcortical parts of the brain. Poised to alert both the higher and lower brain areas, these two structures 'tag' sensory input when something emotionally significant happens, activating important brain nuclei that release neurotransmitters. These neurotransmitters (such as norepinephrine, cortisol, dopamine, and acetylcholine) sharpen the senses and create a highly aroused mental state.

If the amygdala tags input as 'good' or safe, then this input will continue on to other regions of your brain for processing. However, if the amygdala tags input as 'bad' or unsafe, an altogether different reaction will occur. If sensory input is tagged as unsafe, then the higher order thinking regions of our brain will be bypassed so that we can quickly respond to the threat. Human brains have evolved to help us survive and thrive, and the amygdala plays a key role here. One can imagine how beneficial this bypassing of higher order thinking was to our ancestors who were hunters and gatherers, indeed there are certain situations in today's world where it is still very helpful. However, in the modern world that which has evolved to save us from immediate danger can also pose its own risks. Whether we are talking about the stress experienced by a prehistoric hunter gatherer faced with an oncoming predator, or that experienced by a modern preschooler faced with an oncoming car, or a peer yelling in their face, the brain's reaction is very similar. The amygdala will tag it as bad and unsafe, resulting in an influx of cortisol and a version of fight, flight, or freeze.

The amygdala and its function will come up again later in this book when we discuss stress. The amygdala also sends emotional information to most areas of the cortex where it is translated into mood, motivation, judgment, and social awareness. It is one of the most relevant brain regions for teachers to understand and be aware of.

The hippocampus

The hippocampus – Greek for seahorse, named for its shape – which is important to learning and memory formation, is another significant part of the limbic system for educators to be aware of. As shown in the diagram above, the hippocampus is situated right next to the amygdala. The hippocampus receives emotional input from the amygdala, contributing to the formation of memories with emotional relevance. It also helps humans process memories related to facts, events, and spatial relationships (like navigation and the relationship of one's body to objects around it). Although short term memories are converted into long-term memories in the hippocampus, they are then stored in the cortex. The hippocampus and the amygdala are essentially wired up by age five, but their connections to the frontal cortex are still maturing at this stage.

The Prefrontal Cortex

The prefrontal cortex is my favorite. Yes, I know how silly that sounds especially since many parts of the brain are active in learning, but I get excited to think about what happens and what has the *potential* to happen in the prefrontal cortex. When we talk about thinking deeply and making unique connections or creations, we are talking about activity in the prefrontal cortex. It is the location of what is considered our *higher order thinking skills*, and has tremendous significance for teaching as it is one of the areas we call upon the most in the act of learning and thinking deeply. It is also the last area of the brain to develop outside of the womb and many are shocked to find out that this area does not typically become fully developed until one's mid to late twenties. However, it is also an important area to know about and help cultivate in the early years of life and school (even though there are many years of development ahead). Let's explore why this is so.

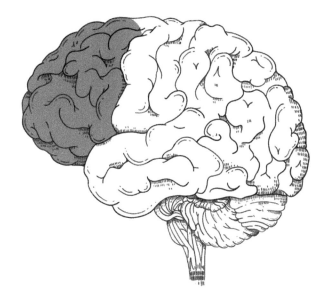

The prefrontal cortex is the region of the brain that has most recently evolved for humans as a species. It is also the last to reach mature development in individuals and is the most plastic. That long period of maturation gives teachers and parents more of a chance to influence how the prefrontal cortex wires up. The neural networks in the prefrontal cortex and the skills and knowledge connected to those networks have a large influence on all other areas of learning and growth in school and beyond. One reason for this is that the structural and functional maturity of the prefrontal cortex play a major role in executive function skills.

Executive functions are a hot topic in education and psychology for good reason. They are a suite of skills that can be separated, but all are understood to share a common purpose. That purpose is 'the allocation of attention and control over behavior, in order to meet an adaptive goal' (Fiske & Holmboe, 2019). Executive functions involve our *working memory* as we hold onto and account for rules and information (for brief amounts of time) in the service of making appropriate or advantageous decisions. They involve *emotion regulation* as the prefrontal cortex communicates with the limbic system so we can respond as opposed to react to emotionally charged situations (i.e. using higher order thinking). It involves *attentional sustaining* and *attentional switching* to focus on our larger purposes despite a myriad of potential distractions. It is our suite of executive function skills that allow for *self-control, self-awareness,* and *cognitive flexibility.*

The three major networks for cognitive processing

Although we have so far focused on learning about specific regions of the brain, there has been a shift among neuroscientists to focus more on the connectivity between regions when looking at aspects of thinking and learning. In other words, there are good reason to look at the 'cross talk' of neurons and how this influences a broad range of mental capacities. This connectivity is generally characterized as three networks: the *executive control network, the default mode network,* and *the salience network.* Each of these networks coordinate with each other and contribute to the social, emotional, and overall cognitive functioning of an individual over their lifespan.

- **The executive control network**
  This is the network recruited in executive functioning (described above).

- **The default mode network**
  This network is recruited during a variety of tasks that involve reflection and internally directed thought (such as remembering, imagining hypothetical scenarios, and daydreaming). Its importance is connected to a person's abilities for conceptual understanding, reading comprehension, creativity, identity development, as well as motivating emotions like admiration, inspiration, and compassion (Immordino-Yang, Darling-Hammond, & Krone, 2018).

- **The salience network**
  This network facilitates the switching from the inwardly directed default mode network to the outwardly directed executive control network. In other words, this is the network we use when attributing relevance or importance to an idea that then necessitates the completion of actions or tasks.

A closer look at the brain in early childhood

A lot is happening in the brain in the years leading up to and during preschool, pre-K, and kindergarten. The brain triples in size during the first year of life and is virtually fully grown by kindergarten. So, although the brain has reached 90% of its adult size by the age of five, it is the changes in neural networks, and more specifically, our synapses, that are the key to our brain development in early childhood. While experience will continue to sculpt the brain into adulthood, early childhood, the height of neural plasticity, is a foundational time.

From infancy to early childhood massive growth of dendrites and synapses among frontal lobe neurons occurs as well as massive pruning. Sensory and motor regions are becoming more efficient and interconnected and, by the age of three, the child has developed a working knowledge of daily routines and familiar environments, as well as increased abilities in social communication, emotion, object manipulation, and understanding time and sequence. Now that the world around them is comfortably familiar, most children at this age begin to take an active role in choosing what they will be curious about. 'The everyday world becomes the familiar background to more distinctive events and objects, which call out for further explanation and mastery' (Engel, 2021). The developing brain shows an explosion of neuronal activity around the age of six.

Children's brains are programmed to learn. The brain forms, refines, and eliminates neural connections according to the influence of genes and experience and each brain is unique (further elaborated upon in the next chapter). The early years have extreme importance for the path these networks will take. That is, early brain development provides a kind of 'organizing template, influencing future growth and development' (Stamm, 2007). The process of learning advances in other ways as the child grows older, especially if the environment and experiences are optimized for learning.

Summary

Brain development happens over time and in many places and contexts including at home and in school. There is an interplay between the individual and their context that is always happening and is expressed as progressive neural integration in our brains. Neural pathways that are used repetitively increase in synaptic strength in the developing brain. This progressive organization and reorganization of our complex brains happens both in childhood and across a lifespan. Teachers have impact on this progressive organization and reorganization of their students' brains.

A mental model of neuroanatomy and how and why the brain changes and develops, empowers the teacher/researcher to make a greater impact, but also to better understand that impact. Knowledge of neurons and how information flows through and between neurons (synaptic connections) to create neural networks that translate into a student's skills and knowledge is powerful. Understanding that part of our job is to help create the conditions that build robust neural networks through varied and repetitive neuronal firing should inform our everyday planning and interactions with students. Knowledge of the limbic system, its role in survival, emotions, memory, and learning as well as the prefrontal cortex and its role in higher order thinking should also inform our practice. Similarly, understanding the importance of connectivity in three major networks (the executive control network, the default mode network, and the salience network), deepens our awareness of the cross talk that happens in the brain that in turn influences children's developing cognitive capacities.

Bolstered by this knowledge, teachers can create optimal experiences that encourage learning so that our students not only acquire complex skills but also gain confidence in their capacity to do so.

Invitation to inquiry

- This chapter describes structures that are developing in the brains of the young children we teach. How does this mental model of the brain and its structures relate to your understanding of child behavior and skill development during this age?
- What is the significance of Hebb's axiom, neurons that fire together wire together?
- How might you approach and interpret the development of skills differently taking account of how neurons grow dendritic connections and myelin?
- In what ways could you be mindful of the limbic system when creating environments in which children feel safe in their identities as small humans and as contributing members of a learning community?
- Can you think of ways in which you can introduce basic neuroanatomy to the children you teach?
- Given a child's prefrontal cortex is developing, can you think of ways to foster the higher order thinking skills of inquiry and theorizing?
- Likewise (still considering the prefrontal cortex), can you think of ways to foster executive function skills such as setting goals, planning, self-monitoring progress, working memory, and cognitive flexibility?

Further reading

Hammond, Zaretta (2015) *Culturally Responsive Teaching & The Brain: Promoting authentic engagement and rigor among culturally and linguistically diverse students.*

CHAPTER 4:
EARLY CHILDHOOD DEVELOPMENT THROUGH AN ANTHROPOLOGICAL LENS

Knowing where something comes from always helps you to understand it.

Allison Gopnik (2016)

Now that we have a background knowledge of the significant structures and functions of the brain, we can deepen our understanding of early childhood brain development by examining it through an anthropological lens. This lens will help us better understand the many facets that make early childhood special and different from other periods of development. And this knowledge, again, will aid our mission of optimizing the conditions for learning and growth for the children we teach.

Early childhood

Knowledge of our evolutionary history helps us understand a great deal about humans today: our biology and why our organs work the way that they do, our behavior and how our minds work, as well as our relationships with the planet, with other species, and with other people. The structure and function of the human brain is very much tied to how it has evolved over time. The evolution of our cultures, concepts of reality, traditions, and notions are interlayered with our physical and physiological adaptations as a species. The story of humans is fascinating and complex. But what does our evolutionary history tell us about childhood specifically?

Modern human beings, or *Homo sapiens sapiens* (also known as just *homo sapiens*), are theorized to have evolved sometime between 160,000 and 90,000 years ago. The characteristics that set them (us) apart from other species were larger brain size, more advanced cognitive abilities, and bipedalism (ability to stand upright and walk on two feet). These physical attributes and capacities increased aptitude for language, for making and iterating tools, and for cooperation, sharing knowledge and resources for the benefit of individuals and groups. An important and significant change in our evolution, that is of particular interest to the topic of early childhood learning, was our relationships with other humans and how this relationship-building behavior affected learning, intelligence, and success.

Relationships are at the heart of learning and development

For prehistoric humans the relationship between children and caretakers was a matter of immediate survival, naturally, but also contributed to stronger societies as a whole. Compared to most other species, human children have an exceptionally long period of immaturity during which they depend upon care from others. It is theorized that human beings with their longer childhoods and relatively larger brain size were positioned to learn more than other creatures. While under the care of adults, human children had advantageous circumstances in which to acquire knowledge, skills, and the ability to adapt quickly to unpredictable conditions.

Being cared for as young children allowed prehistoric humans to learn from exploration and discovery as well as each other. This is still how young children learn. Human adults dedicate remarkably large amounts of time and energy into taking care of and teaching our youth. Relationships and learning during childhood have crucial implications not only for individuals but also to humans *as a species*. It has been to the benefit of our species that we take extra time in both growing our brains (biology) and in intentionally optimizing their development to thrive (pedagogy). Today, as in prehistory, children are taken care of by multiple adults and all of the adults in a child's life have a corresponding impact. As educators of young children, we are essential agents in the story of their learning and growing.

Our longer childhood and the relationships we have with caretakers and teachers have evolved alongside our adaptive abilities to learn and grow. In the simplest of terms, children learn from other people as well as through discovery and exploration. We all know that learning takes time: for trial and error, to learn from mistakes, to practice (and practice, and practice), and to build robust neural networks. All this time makes us somewhat vulnerable in the world. However, in a society in which one feels safe, not under threat from encroaching mammoths or other more modern forms of harm and isolation, children can do what they have evolved to do, to learn and grow.

The human impulse to explore to understand is never more powerful than it is in early childhood. This, in and of itself, is a powerful statement and has profound implications for educators and parents. If this is part of what makes us successful as a species, it should be tremendously important when we think of learning, growth, and compulsory education. The four driving motivations of our childhood need to understand the world are: to connect to others, explore, imagine, and innovate. These four motivations are profoundly connected to happiness, identity, and the pursuit of purpose. They are also connected to a disposition of mind.

To explore, imagine, and innovate

Children are 'the most capable learners on the planet' (Spelke & Sutts, 2020). Through exploring objects, environments, materials, and ideas, children learn about the world, themselves, who they are in relation to others, and the possibilities open to them. As a species, humans are explorers. While history provides many examples of how this has been both good and bad for the earth and its inhabitants, it still remains an important part of the human story. While many other species have adapted to their particular environments, we have been nomads that wander, discover, and find ways to survive and sometimes, thrive. Through exploring, imagining, and innovating, humans have figured out how to live almost anywhere from the coldest to the hottest environments, from dry and barren to abundantly verdant landscapes, from the most populous to the most isolated of locations. Imagination and exploration are intimately connected. Think of how a scientist, for example, might move between exploration, imagination, and innovation when testing a hypothesis. They might start with imagining a connection or reaction, then move to exploration through designed experiments, which could then lead to innovation in different forms. Think of what a jazz musician does before, during, and after their time on stage. Think of what a veteran teacher might do to reach a student that is struggling in the moment, either academically or socially. And think of what a child does as they play. Young children do these things naturally, but they still need to be fostered, supported, and given the literal and figurative space to develop. This is true of all humans. To explore, imagine, and innovate, we need to develop skills, dispositions, mindsets, and knowledge. This is only possible if we have the time and safe space to develop them.

Allison Gopnik has developed a very useful framework for understanding early childhood learning and development. According to Gopnik, childhood is characterized by *exploration*, and this is supported by the developing brain structures. Remember that during childhood, the developing brain has many more synaptic connections, and greater potential for plasticity. Adulthood, on the other hand, is marked by *exploitation*; adults exploit their existing knowledge through more focused attention and efficient use of resources and skills. This is also supported by mature brain structures. The more mature brain has pruned away neural networks and has created 'information superhighways.' Young brains have evolved to explore knowledge while mature brains have evolved to exploit it. A corollary of this is that healthy development in children requires the time and space to be 'intellectually messy, to explore before they can exploit' (Gopnik, 2016) – a description I am sure will seem apt to anyone working with young learners day in and day out.

How does innovation fit into this framework? Each generation is met with new circumstances and challenges so while there is always much to learn from adults and elders, there is also a necessary and predictable generational need to innovate. The period of time between childhood and early adulthood is essentially a time of learning from adults while making adaptations and innovations. As Gopnik puts it, 'our human evolutionary inheritance crucially includes the ability to overthrow or revise that very inheritance' (Gopnik, 2016). Children, young and old, have always learned from the adults around them while also feeling compelled to make their own mark. The children in your classroom similarly need to learn from you and the other educators in the school while also making their own mark.

Summary

This chapter is an overview of early childhood learning and development through an anthropological lens. We have looked at the evolutionary history of childhood, part of which is the crucial relationships children have with their caretakers as they construct knowledge and meaning in the world. I have highlighted four human motivational drives: to connect with others, explore, imagine, and innovate. These drives are what make children such capable learners, predisposed for learning by exploring their environment and engaging with other humans. This is why children need to be given agency and opportunities to be creative and imaginative. As Gopnik puts it, childhood is marked by exploration and this drive is reflected in the developing neural circuitry of children. In contrast adulthood is marked by exploitation, and this is also reflected in the neural circuitry of adults. With this background knowledge we can better understand aspects of our work as educators as we attempt to optimize learning. *How* young children learn is also at the core of what *motivates* children to learn. Fostering motivation for learning leads us back to dispositions of mind.

> **Invitation to inquiry**
>
> - Are there specific reasons why you were drawn to teaching this age group? What were/are they?
> - How can we use young children's natural drives for social connection, exploration, innovation, and creativity to foster a positive disposition of mind towards learning?

Further reading

Dehaene, Stanislas (2021) *How We Learn: Why brains learn better than any machine … for now.*

Gopnik, Alison (2016) *The Gardener and the Carpenter: What the New Science of Child Development Tells Us About the Relationship Between Parents and Children.*

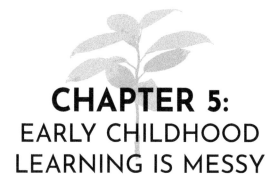

CHAPTER 5:
EARLY CHILDHOOD LEARNING IS MESSY

Everyone should learn to happily make errors ...To think is to move from one error to the next.

Émile Chartier Alain (1932)

Individuals do not develop merely by existing, or growing older, or becoming larger; they must undergo certain pivotal experiences that result in periodic reorganizations of their knowledge and their understanding.

Howard Gardner (1990)

Learning is messy. There are several reasons for this. Development happens quickly and across many domains in early childhood. Children can appear to have surprising competencies in one area on one day, and then exhibit surprising incompetency in other areas on other days. At the same time, young children like to test cause and effect, and 'hands on' learning can lead to messy mistakes. Further, young children are just beginning to learn how to recognize and label emotions (and that is only if they are explicitly taught) as well as how to regulate them. Through all of this 'mess', teachers are looking for patterns and probabilities that will help them understand the child and how to scaffold their learning path. Teachers want to measure progress and that is easier when there is order, neat rows and columns that can be checked off. But just as we have to embrace the complexity of learning and development, we also have to go into this endeavor with an understanding of the inherent and inevitable messiness of it.

'The purpose of education should be to develop and extend the talents and potential in each child' (Cantor, et al, 2021). We cannot know a child's potential as a learner in advance. Recall that genes are chemical followers and experience plays a major role in gene expression. Likewise, experiences (especially relationships) will continuously affect development in dynamic ways. We can, however, use what we do know about each student and about the science of learning to enhance strengths and address weaknesses.

Another reason why learning is messy is because each contributing factor in a child's spheres of influence from the micro to the macro (their identity, age, family background, health, culture, socio-economic and socio-historical background, etc.), as varied as they may be, are still part of that individual's developmental story. In the brain this is reflected by how neural networks are anatomically cross-wired and integrated, not separated as distinct parts that can then be controlled. These myriad factors are reciprocally influential and interconnected. Therefore, it is rare that we will be able to isolate one reason to explain a behavior or skill and more likely we will be looking at a set of possible interconnected reasons.

Another explanation of the beautiful messiness of learning has to do with the amount of it that is happening simultaneously. David Elkind (2007) uses the analogy of visiting a foreign country to describe childhood education. This foreign country is full of human behavior, societal expectations, relationships, concepts, even objects that are new and strange to the child.

> During the first years of their lives young children are quite literally visiting a foreign country. And, because young children do not think in adult concepts and categories, they approach this new land from many different perspectives at the same time. They see this new world as an artist, naturalist, writer, scientist, and much more.

I agree wholeheartedly with Dr. Elkind that this is one of the reasons why observing young children make sense of their world is so utterly fascinating.

Early childhood, variability, and adaptability

Children are not all the same. Just as variability and change are part of our evolutionary history as a species, they are very much a part of who we are as individuals and how we adapt and develop. An anthropologist would explain that variability is what allows our species to survive when things change. Similarly, between individuals, temperaments, abilities, interests, development, and personal biographies will always vary.

Childhood is meant to be an extended period of variability and possibility, of inquiry and creativity, of learning, growth, and imagination. This long, complex childhood filled with both predictable and unpredictable behaviors contributes to human evolvability (i.e. the capacity for adaptive evolution). We will return to the topic of epigenetics – the study of how your behaviors and environment can cause changes that affect the way your genes work – in the following chapter, but as we think of young learners, it is important to remember that factors that contribute to complexity and disorder in childhood development also contribute to diversity and variability, and that these are rules in human development, not exceptions. Disorder is not something that needs to be controlled, but it does need to be understood.

Variability does not just arise in physical features, temperament, interest, and personal biographies. Individual children acquire skills in varied ways at different times. This *when* and *how* will directly impact how the teacher chooses to introduce and scaffold content and skills. To make matters even more complex, an individual child will perform the same individual skill variably. If we understand *skill* to be a person's ability to exert control over thinking, feeling, and acting, we also understand that this happens within a particular sociocultural context. The performance of any skill, especially a newly formed skill, can vary greatly between home, the classroom, the playground, in front of peers, etc. In other words, broad contextual factors will contribute to variability of skill acquisition and performance. This is why no single measure (like an assessment or test) can accurately represent the level of a particular skill for a particular student. Quite simply, a single measure cannot reflect the variability of performance due to contextual factors. In addition, how we direct a child's attention during a task – how we scaffold – and whether the child feels a sense of efficacy will greatly influence how that child performs. This is why there are distinct levels of competence under different levels of support, what Bloom and Vygotsky referred to as *developmental range*. Teachers know this and it is why we are always looking for ways to help children that are taking different pathways towards skill acquisition and performance.

The ubiquity of variability is essential for educators to grasp. Skill development is 'jagged', i.e. variable and dependent on context. Moving away from the idea that there are dependable, predictable patterns of intelligence, learning 'styles', fixed stages of development, or easily defined and identifiable endpoints may be hard to embrace but is necessary to better understand how we can help children learn. With variability in mind, we can better design learning environments that can respond to the fundamental jaggedness of skill development and assess, respond to, and scaffold, individual learning trajectories with greater understanding and accuracy.

Learning trajectories

Skill and competency development are not discrete, linear, and reliably measurable because growth trajectories are not predictable. Human development is a process with peaks and valleys and the pace, direction, and quality of the development will naturally vary just as each person's experiences in the world vary (Rose, 2016). What this means for educators is that the acquisition of skills and knowledge is inherently and profoundly nonlinear. Skills will often develop in fits and starts, with forward progress followed by backward movement before going forward again. And while individuals will follow a jagged course, there will also be variation *among* learners. Each child will have a different jagged course. Sometimes, backward movement might be due to consolidation that is happening at a lower level of a complex skill. Sometimes, it is because a connecting dimension of the skill is not yet mastered. Sometimes, it is the influence of external factors or experiences that alter the trajectory of skill acquisition.

This is not to say that we should not teach in systematic ways with more complex skills building upon less complex skills. We should often teach this way, especially with literacy and numeracy! However, we cannot expect that children's learning trajectories and achievements will be as linear as our lesson plans.

Another salient point here is that *because* each child has a developmental range of competency, no one score can adequately represent the breadth of their knowledge, abilities, and potential. Unfortunately, formal education was designed upon the faulty premise that we all progress in predictable lock-step patterns and that scores can tell us the whole story of what one knows and can know. This premise persists today in schools and classrooms everywhere. However, the true nature of human development and learning is integrated, dynamic, and individual.

Dynamic Systems Theory

Human development happens over time and in many places and contexts. While this development is occurring, the brain is changing, and becoming increasingly connected and integrated. This growing capacity to make sense of the world, form healthy relationships, and acquire complex skills, in turn allows children to explore, make meaning, and understand the world around them. Micro-developmental processes (smaller scale skills) converge and integrate with macro-developmental processes (larger scale skills) and then stabilize over time. Long and short-term change occurs simultaneously as the learner accumulates experiences, skills, and knowledge.

According to the Dynamic Systems Theory, each child is an integrated dynamic system with almost infinite potentialities. Cantor, et al, (2021) state, 'whole-child development, learning, and thriving emerge from the malleability, agency, and *developmental range* of a child' as they draw from an interconnected web of relations and experiences across all parts of their lives. This conception of a web of dynamic factors influencing growth and development presents both opportunities and vulnerabilities.

The goal of the educator and the educational system is to provide well-designed environments and pedagogies that aim to:

- Drive the expression of each child's genetic endowment and epigenetic attributes.
- Harness the malleability of their bodies and brains.
- Nurture the fullest expression of what each child becomes.

Inherent in this theory is the understanding that children possess a broad set of potentialities across multiple domains. The role of the educator is 'not to teach discrete skills, but to create opportunities for each child to want to bring parts of their interests, passions, talents, prior experiences, culture, and existing capability to bear' (Cantor, et al, 2021).

Connecting the brain to the rest of the body

The brain does not grow and develop outside of the body that homes it. Rather, the brain, as with all other biological systems in the body, develops alongside and is connected to the other organs and systems, such as the heart and lung systems, digestion, energy production, immune response, and physical growth. These organs and systems interact with and inform each other, adapting to the contexts in which the child is developing as a team. 'Each system 'reads' the environment, prepares to respond, and shares that information with the others. Each system then 'signals back' to the others through feedback loops already functioning at birth' (Shonkoff, et al, 2020). These systems are responsible for lifelong health and well-being, and they are also connected to learning. The body's biological systems including the brain's developing circuits, are sensitive to adversity and stress. There are three main areas in which the brain is susceptible to high levels of chronic stress in early childhood:

- Emotion regulation.
- Memory systems.
- Executive function systems.

Young children experiencing high levels of chronic stress often exhibit strong emotional responses (especially associated with a perceived threat), struggles with memory as well as impulse control, and difficulties with other higher-level cognitive skills during lessons. The good news is that children and their developing brains are also sensitive to warm and responsive relationships, a culture of care and safety, and consistent routines. Healthy relationships with teachers in a caring environment with peers in which 'serve and return' interactions are plentiful can reduce stress activation and protect the developing systems of children.

Summary

This chapter hopefully illustrates why we should embrace the 'messiness' of early childhood learning. And, perhaps, the mess won't seem so messy if it is, in fact, what we expect. The complexity of learning and development allows for incredible potential growth, but also explains the multi-layered causes and conditions for the behaviors and skill development we see in children. We can create linear and systematic lesson plans, but the consolidation of knowledge and skills in children will not always follow a predictable and linear pattern. Human development happens over time and in many places and contexts and while development is occurring, the brain is changing. Variability and adaptability are the rules of human development, not the exceptions. Brain development is interconnected to the development of other vital biological systems in the body. Excessive stress impedes healthy growth and development in the brain and the body, but safe environments and healthy relationships counteract the harms of stress. Keeping the messiness of learning in mind, we can provide strong teacher-student relationships and well-designed environments to support the well-being of individuals and their learning trajectories.

Invitation to inquiry

- The non-linear and unpredictable nature of skill development and learning poses challenges to teachers when designing curricula, lessons, and assessments. Given that schools and classrooms differ greatly, what are some ways to overcome these challenges?

- Variability and adaptability are linked in human evolution as well as skill development. Variability can certainly make our job more complicated, but what are some of the upsides?

- The Dynamic Systems Theory underscores the complexity of child development and learning. Thinking of one specific student, can you list multiple factors that would influence the development of a chosen skill, say for example, oral expressive language or spatial reasoning?

Further reading

Darling-Hamond, L., Cantor, P., Hernandez, L. E., Schachner, S. P., Theokas, C., and E. Tijerina (2020) *Guiding principles for equitable Whole-Child Design.* Available at: https://turnaroundusa.org/whole-child-design-principles/.

Bronfenbrenner, U. (1979) *The Ecology of Human Development; Experiments by Nature and Design.*

Bronfenbrenner, U. (1986) 'Ecology of the Family as a Context for Human Development'. *Research Perspectives Developmental Psychology.* 22: 723-742. DOI: 10.1037/0012-1649.22.6.723

CHAPTER 6:
EARLY CHILDHOOD AND MIND, BRAIN, AND EDUCATION

To be a teacher in the right sense is to be a learner. Instruction begins when you, the teacher, learn from the learner, put yourself in his place so that you may understand what he understands and the way he understands it.

Soren Kierkegaard

As the brain's neural pathways become increasingly connected and integrated in response to the child's experiences, these changes increase their ability to make sense of the world. Given supportive learning experiences, these brain changes will also help the child form healthy relationships, and acquire complex skills which in turn, helps them understand and make decisions about how they want to be in the world. This is why our work as educators is inextricably linked to an understanding of how the brain learns and develops (and the myriad factors that influence it).

Learning in the brain is complex and a range of disciplines are necessary to appreciate the full picture. This chapter brings together Mind, Brain, and Education (MBE) concepts that are foundational for understanding early childhood education. Each of these disciplines contributes to our understanding of teaching, learning, and child development and provides ideas that can be translated into our classrooms. As Howard Gardner observes, 'None of them [Mind, Brain, and Education] is definitive, but it would be foolish to ignore any of them, and we are best off if we try to draw on the range of perspectives, paying particular attention when the various indices point in the same direction' (quoted in Immordino-Yang, 2016).

As with all sciences, theories in MBE evolve rapidly and keeping abreast of current research is close to impossible for most classroom teachers. Likewise, it can be challenging and time-consuming translating research findings into applied strategies that have applicable and positive impact in actual classrooms with actual students. Another challenge is the proliferation of 'neuromyths' – that is misconceptions, untruths, or misinterpreted findings that get marketed to educators as 'what works' – such as the discredited but widely accepted idea of 'learning styles'. There are trustworthy and up-to-date organizations that exist to help teachers sift through the research: The Center for Transformative Teaching and Learning, The Education Endowment Foundation, and The Harvard Center of the Developing Child. Despite the challenges, knowledge of MBE is something all teachers of any grade should have.

Chapter three covered the basics of neuroanatomy to help the reader build a mental model of the brain, neural networks, neurons, and the synapses. Much of what we understand about the brain and its physical structures, functions, and development comes from neuroscience. Neuroscientists study the energy flow of the brain via brain imaging. Imaging allows us to see how the brain consumes energy and how processes of arousal and activation within the brain directly shape neural circuitry. The brain's developing circuitry reflects an individual's social, emotional, and cognitive experiences and these circuits and mental processes become linked and integrated into a functional whole. Brain imaging affords us the ability to literally see how the whole becomes different from the sum of its parts.

This chapter covers the foundational MBE concepts most helpful for understanding learning in early childhood and those that have the most potential impact in the classroom.

- Neuroplasticity and Hebb's axiom.
- Adaptive Epigenesis.
- Executive Functions.
- Attention.

- Memory.
- Motivation.
- Learning Through Play (see chapter seven).
- Emotion and Cognition (see chapter eight).
- Social Cognition (see chapter nine).

Neuroplasticity

In her book, *Neuromyths*, Tracey Tokuhama-Espinosa identifies broadly accepted and research-supported principles and tenets about our brains and how we learn. Her work emphasizes the basic truth that while no two brains are identical, we can understand the significant differences better if we appreciate their significant commonalities. While genetic makeup plays a key role in brain development, relationships, environments, and experiences – both positive and negative – are the primary determinants of learning and development. And that is why the concept of neuroplasticity is the most important, and perhaps, the most foundational MBE concept of all. Simply put, *neuroplasticity* is the ability of the brain to change over time. While brain change is possible throughout our lives, there are stages in which there is greater plasticity and early childhood is one of them.

Brain change looks different in adults than in young children. As discussed in the previous chapter, the brains of young children are going through a process of organization, integration, neurogenesis, and pruning that looks similar across children of the same age. For most young children, these predictable developmental changes are occurring while, simultaneously, new neural networks are being created.

Remember Hebb's axiom? *Neurons that fire together wire together.* Put another way, the power of repetition for learning is that repeated experiences not only create neural networks, but they also contribute to the myelination that makes these connections more robust and efficient. This process leads to the development of more complex skills. As early childhood educators, it is important that we understand that such circuits developed in early childhood can form the functional basis for enduring patterns later in life (Immoridno-Yang & Demasio, 2007; Siegel, 2020).

Skills do not just appear in a person's repertoire. Teachers that learn about neuroplasticity and the power of building neural networks through experience and repetition will never see skill acquisition the same way. The advancement of a skill or a conceptual understanding is fundamentally the building up of neural networks. Knowledge and skills are built up gradually over time and with practice of real activities in real contexts. It is important to remember that the bidirectional influences between an individual and their contexts means that there are multiple pathways that developmental change can take. This also means that just because a behavior is demonstrated at one point in time does not necessarily mean that it will be repeated later. However, neuroplasticity (the ability of our brains to change), and Hebb's axiom (the mechanism by which neural networks are built), are reasons for optimism for human development and learning; there is always the potential for thriving if environments and systems are designed for it.

Adaptive epigenesis

Epigenetics – derived from 'epi', the Greek for over – is the concept that there are influencers that go 'over' or 'above' the effect of genes. *Epigenetic adaptation* (or adaptive epigenesis) is a biological process that influences learning, behavior, neural integration, and health. Our development over the course of our lives depends upon the interaction of our genes with our environment, relationships, and experiences. Genes encode *potential*. They are like packages of biological instructions that require signals to determine if and when processes are carried out and how they will be expressed. The human genome is made up of approximately 20,000 genes. There are many proteins which are involved in the process of transcribing DNA into RNA (Cantor, et al, 2021), and through this mechanism the environment and experiences of an individual create chemical signals that affect gene expression. One of the most fascinating aspects of epigenetics is that this process begins before conception via parental experiences, cultures, and histories. Qualitative changes in genetic makeup can be passed on within and across generations (Cantor, et al, 2021). A person's ability to thrive emerges from the interconnectedness of biological, physiological, cultural, and historical systems. This field of epigenetics within MBE is bound to enthrall, enlighten, and inform those interested in the science of learning.

Executive functions

We discussed executive functions in chapter three (see p. 62) because it is hard to talk about the prefrontal cortex and its significance without also talking about executive functions. To recap, executive functions include the complex abilities to:

- Deliberately inhibit certain behaviors and act upon others.
- Weigh options and make decisions.
- Set goals and plan actions accordingly.
- Monitor progress.

The prefrontal cortex itself is fully functional from birth, but its decision-making neural networks are not well rehearsed. This means that it is highly susceptible to influences from the environment – hence it's high degree of neuroplasticity. As discussed in chapter three, executive functioning skills include working memory, emotion regulation, higher order thinking, attentional sustaining, attentional switching, self-control, self-awareness, and cognitive flexibility. Research supports correlations between strong executive function skills and:

- School readiness and performance, as well as future success in life (Diamond, 2013).
- Better performance in mathematics (Bull, Expy, & Weibe, 2008; Clark, Pritchard, & Woodward, 2010).
- Greater language abilities (Follmer, 2018).
- Prosocial behaviors. Children's social play is believed to be an important practice ground for executive function skill development (Eisenberg et al, 2004).

Everyone benefits from better executive functioning skills. Let's help students build them. While to date, there is no one strategy that definitively enhances all executive function skills, there are programs that show promise. Executive function skills 'can be improved – at every age from infancy through old age' (Diamond & Ling, 2019). Classroom strategies that promote executive function skill growth include developing strong relationships with children using necessary scaffolding and co-regulation of emotions, and providing ample opportunities for children to practice self-directed activities that incorporate meta-cognition and/or self-monitoring.

Attention

While we are all born with the ability to be alert, directing our attention and controlling it is a behavior that is developed over time. We cannot possibly pay attention to all of the sensory input we are exposed to, and the brains of young children are developing ways to manage attention to avoid chaos. As Kelleher and Whitman point out in their book, *Neuroteach*, people often think of a lack of attention is reflective of the child's respect towards the subject or teacher when in fact, 'attention refers to a semiautomatic brain system that helps people manage the flow of information entering their brains, and is not necessarily something they can control'. The neuronal wiring needed for attention unfolds partly naturally and partly as a response to experience and environment. One key factor in attention is safety. Safety does not just refer to physical safety; children must know that they are not in harm's way emotionally, socially, and physically. If a child does not feel safe and secure, their brain cannot attend to anything else.

According to psychologist Michael Posner, there are three components to the attention system. To pay attention, you must: *alert* yourself to something, *shift* your focus to that thing, and lastly, *maintain* your focus. While alerting and shifting wires up early in brain development (within the first 14 months after birth), the third component develops much more slowly. Maintaining attention despite competing stimuli requires inhibitory response (and is one of the executive function skills).

Memory

While memory is largely associated with the limbic system (specifically, the hippocampus), it is in fact not a single entity but a patchwork of several different forms of information storage that develop slowly in conjunction with different brain circuits. The profound lack of memory in infancy and early childhood, often referred to by psychologists as *infantile amnesia*, fully wanes around age five or six. Memory storage increases throughout preschool and into elementary years when children become aware of their own memory and use mnemonic strategies to help them acquire and retain more information. The entire nervous system participates in making memories.

Memory is categorized into levels starting from our *basic familiarity* with our environment. From there, our memory skills progress to *rote memory, working memory* (short-term memory), patterning and connections to *relational memory*, and ultimately, *long-term memory* storage (Willis, 2006). Rote memory, often associated with test taking, is a type of learning that involves quick forgetting. This is because facts that are rehearsed over and over don't form elaborate connections of neurons. 'With nothing to give them context or relationship to each other or to the students' lives, these facts are stored in remoter areas of the brain' (Willis, 2006). With few neuronal pathways, these isolated bits of information are hard to access with future cues.

Working memory refers to the information that we store for use in the immediate future. The goal is to transfer that information into long-term memory storage before it is forgotten entirely. If children can make their own connections to previously learned material or experience, or see patterns, then their working memory is more likely to become long-term memory. There are many ways in which educators of three to six-year-olds can help them to develop short-term memories into long-term memories. For example, if a child is asked to draw or sketch what she has just learned and then verbally communicate it, the child will be building stronger memory circuits. The intentional use of novelty, play, emotion, purpose, hands-on activities, active retrieval, and interleaving are all strategies that teachers can use to help children store information in long-term memory.

There are many other forms of memory. Relational memory refers to associations between two things, say for example, names and faces. Relational memory can also refer to location, order, or context. Recognition memory is exactly what it sounds like – the ability to recognize that a phenomenon has previously occurred, and you are seeing or experiencing it again. Recognition memory improves significantly in preschool years, and this is perhaps related to the myelination and synaptic refinement occurring at this time. Spatial memory and visual spatial memory are the faculties used in games like Memory. Five-year-olds tend to be particularly good with memory for object locations. Verbal recall – which is considered the last memory milestone for children – improves dramatically in preschool years, closely paralleling developments in language.

Memories can also be categorized by type in a more descriptive fashion as is the case when we distinguish between episodic, semantic, and procedural memories. Episodic memories refer to particular events or episodes in one's life, for example, the child's first day of school. These memories are processed in different brain areas than semantic memories such as names, numbers, dates, and facts. Lastly, procedural memory gives us the ability to remember and perform a skill, once again a distinct type of memory using different parts of the brain.

We know that the more ways a subject is taught in class, the more dendritic pathways (i.e. connections between the dendrites) will be created, and the better the memory storage and access generated will be. As Willis (2006) puts it:

> ... offering the information visually will set up connections with the occipital lobes (the posterior lobes of the brain that process optical input). Subsequently or simultaneously having students hear the information will hook up a dendritic circuit with the temporal lobes (the lobes on the sides of the brain that process auditory input and play an important role in the regulation of emotion and memory processing).

Establishing multiple pathways give greater opportunity for future cues to prompt access to this stored information.

Motivation

While one could spend hundreds of pages discussing the topic of human motivation, I want to explicitly highlight a few aspects that are relevant to early childhood education, although ideas surrounding motivation are referenced throughout this book. Because the brain is the organ for learning and we all have brains, there is a built-in motivation for learning. However, remember that the brain is a metabolically expensive tissue in terms of the energy it uses. So, what motivates us to spend time on learning about some things as opposed to others? There are a few basic concepts that are relevant to all humans.

Beginning in infancy, humans are motivated by *novelty* (anything new or something that changes). The other side of novelty is *habituation*. Habituation is the tendency to lose interest in an event or phenomena that is constant or repetitive. Habituation is necessary so that we can develop focused attention on what matters. In early childhood classrooms, we want children to become habituated to the classroom's physical space, routines, and expectations. However, when we want them to get excited about a curricular topic, we need to exploit their novelty preference. Novelty preference develops into curiosity and the motivation to understand the world (Ostroff, 2012), and this is why never-before-seen objects or events are so compelling to young children.

Children, like adults, enjoy the feeling of 'being good at something' and this has an adaptive significance as it propels further cognitive growth. While we are motivated by a good challenge, we also need to have a sense of *self-efficacy*: the belief that with persistence we can accomplish our goals and receive that reward of 'I did it.' These experiences give children confidence to take on future challenges and contribute to their overall sense of self-confidence.

In addition to novelty and self-efficacy, the motivational forces of play, emotion, relevance, purpose, agency, and belonging cannot be overstated when it comes to learning. We will return to these ideas throughout this book. Children are motivated by *fun* and their intrinsic desire to explore, understand, and play (see the following chapter on learning through play). Children's *emotions* are also intricately linked to their motivation and cognition (see chapter eight). Children seek *relevance* and *purpose* and are motivated by meaningful learning experiences. Education has more meaning and relevance when children see the connection to who they are, what they know, and what they are interested in (see chapter nine). Children need to have a sense of agency and are motivated to express themselves. This is why there are chapters on creativity, imagination, and care (chapters twelve and thirteen). There are ways teachers can design individual lessons or units with motivation in mind. Fostering children's *abiding* intellectual curiosity and creativity is about igniting a *lasting motivation* that I refer to as a disposition of mind.

Summary

The field of Mind, Brain, and Education (MBE) provides a framework of concepts that have the power to enhance teaching and learning in both our classroom practice and professional and personal development. Within MBE, there is a spectrum from concepts that are robustly supported by research on one end, to those that show some promise on the other. In our attempts to understand the internal (neuroanatomy, genetics, and epigenetics) and external (pedagogy, experience, and environment) conditions of child development, it is tempting to oversimplify where we can. However, we need to fully embrace the complexity of learning and development while gaining as much insight as we can about our individual students. This chapter attempts to lay out some MBE foundational truths related to neuroplasticity, the role of the environment, executive functions, attention, and memory. These are the foundations for understanding the themes that I believe to be most relevant to early childhood education: play, emotion and cognition, our social brain, the value of classroom conversations, intellectual curiosity, creativity and imagination, balance, and a culture of care.

Invitation to inquiry

Given the concept of neuroplasticity and Hebb's axiom (*neurons that fire together wire together*), how can your classroom practice allow for:

- Repetition of concepts and skills so children can build their neural networks.
- A variety of experiences and modalities so that the neural networks are robustly connected?

Further reading

Tokuhama-Espinosa, Tracey (2018) *Neuromyths: Debunking false ideas about the brain.*

Agarwal, Pooja K. and Parice M. Bain (2019) *Powerful Teaching: Unleash the science of learning.*

Watson, Andrew C. (2021) *The Goldilocks Map: A classroom teacher's quest to evaluate 'brain-based' teaching advice.*

PART 3:
ZOOMING IN

CHAPTER 7:
LEARNING THROUGH PLAY

Combinatory play seems to be the essential feature in productive thought.

Albert Einstein (1945)

Indeed, if there is one fundamental function of play, it is to contribute to the growth of a flexible brain that is primed for creative thinking and problem solving.

Scott Barry Kaufman and Carolyn Gregoire (2015)

The sheer ubiquity of play suggests that it serves important functions. While play is commonly found in social animals, this is especially true for those creatures with longer childhoods, parental investment, and large brains. Creatures like us! 'From a biological, evolutionary perspective, play is nature's way of ensuring that young mammals, including young humans, will practice and become good at the skills they need to develop to survive and thrive in their environments' (Gray, 2013). Play happens only after basic needs for survival such as food, shelter, and social connection, are met. However, once those basic needs are met, humans find ways to play.

To be an educator of young children without taking a serious look at the research and thinking around play would be a grand mistake for play is the dominant mode of learning in early childhood. Many scholars of early childhood education have voiced this general opinion (even if they have disagreed on strategies and specifics), including Froebel, Gesell, Bruner, Erikson, Elkind, Dewey, Piaget, Vygtosky, Badrova and Leong, De Vries, Fein, and Singer and Singer. That is quite a list.

The word 'play' is often associated with the word 'childhood'. Most parents and educators understand that play is a 'good thing,' but might not know how to explain that thinking. Most would even assert that play is a legitimate right for all children, everywhere. Some parents worry that their children are playing too much while others worry that their children are playing too little.

Since the early 2000s, there has been an increased interest in the use of play in early childhood education curricula across several different countries, including Canada, Sweden, China, the United Arab Emirates, and New Zealand (Pyle & Danniels, 2016). One reason for this is that essential elements of play align with optimal conditions for learning. Based on Mind, Brain, and Education research, Hirsh-Pasek, Zosh, and colleagues (2015) have proposed four pillars to describe how humans learn best. Children are primed to learn when they are:

- Mentally active in discovering new knowledge.
- Engaged (as opposed to distracted).
- Interacting with material in ways that are meaningful.
- Socially interactive.

Since all four of these pillars are naturally found in play, it just makes sense as a pedagogical approach.

Definitions and categories of play

So, what *is* play? Given how essential it is to the human story, it is surprisingly difficult to define. Play researchers have offered different definitions. For our discussion, I will use one overarching and simple definition, which we can then elaborate by offering descriptions of play categories and subcategories.

Play is an enjoyable activity that includes variation and choice.

Children learn through play, but the key to this chapter is understanding how different *kinds* of play can serve different learning goals. There is no one type of play that benefits all sorts of learning. With that in mind, let's now define some specific kinds of play and their relationships to learning.

Some researchers use two broad terms to categorize play: structured play and unstructured play. Structured play refers to play that has a specific objective or set of rules and can be directed by teachers or a combination of students and teachers. Unstructured play refers to child-directed play and aligns more closely with the concept of free play. I prefer to use three broad categories instead of two, which exist along a continuum in which free play is on one end and guided play is on the other.

Which type of play experience you design for depends on the objective.

Child-directed.
Teachers are observing and maintaining safety.

Child and Teacher collaborating on goals and objectives of the play experience.

Teacher-directed.
These experiences have more specific learning objectives.

David Elkind (who has his own categories) insightfully notes that this sort of division of play into neat subgroups is artificial, and that intellectual, social, and emotional learning occurs at the same time regardless of the kind play. However, categories are useful to adults as we interpret and understand the value of both play's intrinsic joy and happiness, and relationship to learning and intellectual curiosity.

Free play

> Young children, especially, have enormous creativity, and whatever's in them rises to the surface during free play.
>
> Erik Erikson, *New York Times*, 1994

Free play is self-directed; the players make all the decisions, and the goals can be modified as they go along. According to Peter Gray, 'The things that children learn through their own initiatives, in free play, cannot be taught in other ways' (2013). It is this kind of play that Friedrich Froebel, the creator of the kindergarten, believed to be the directing mode of learning. Other play researchers have proposed that free play allows for explorations of materials and concepts that aid in the construction of knowledge and problem-solving skills. This kind of play has also been associated with improving children's attention by allowing them to release excess energy. It has also been seen as a 'buffer to stressful events and anxiety' as studies have shown a marked decrease in anxiety after periods of free play (Ostroff, 2012). Free play is the means by which children engage with peers and ideas as they learn to make friends, solve problems, and overcome fears in self-directed ways.

Mutually directed play

Next on the continuum is mutually directed play, which is when both teachers and children contribute important ideas about the experience, goals, and direction of the play. Teachers get involved without taking control and do not have specific goals or outcomes in mind other than the observation and possible documentation of play behaviors and skills practiced. This could be accomplished by intentionally designing the play environment and providing certain materials to promote certain skills, child groupings, and topics.

Guided play

Guided play has a greater degree of teacher support and scaffolding. The main difference between mutually directed play and guided play is that the latter is usually designed by teachers for the development of specific learning outcomes. An example of this would be a math board game in which children roll dice and move along a numbered path. The teacher might be targeting the practice of specific skills such as subitizing (recognizing quantity in dots), recognizing numerals, cardinality, or adding on. However, even within guided play, children must have some choice over their actions for it to still be considered play.

There is increasing evidence that free play and guided play contribute to different developmental outcomes (Pyle, 2016). Whereas free play is largely associated with well-being and the development of generalized cognitive abilities such as social competencies, creative problem-solving, and self-regulation, guided play is associated with the acquisition of academic skills. All three categories of play should be thoughtfully incorporated into early childhood education.

Below are two other subcategories of play – exploratory and dramatic (or pretend) play – that I include because 1) there is robust research about them, 2) they are ubiquitous, and 3) they can be both appreciated and leveraged in the early childhood education setting.

Exploratory play

Exploratory play can occur during free, mutually directed, or guided play. It offers a safe space for active observation or data collecting and experimentation. Teachers need to not only support but encourage self-directed exploration. This is because even if the activity appears meaningless to us, it likely has great purpose or significance to the child and the concept building that is occurring in their brain. It is exceptionally hard for adults to think like a three to six-year-old, but we have to remember that a child's exploration has a pattern and an organization in keeping with that child's mental development. Allowing and creating these opportunities nourishes that child's powers of concentration and attention. This is why close observation and documentation by the teacher is as important as their flexibility to follow the lead of the child. This is not the same thing as saying leave kids alone and they will learn best, nor is this the approach known as *exploratory learning.* The role of the educator in observing, documenting, and scaffolding is what makes exploratory play a powerful tool in the design of educational experiences in early childhood.

Dramatic play

This type of play goes by many names: socio-dramatic play, pretend play, pretense play, and imaginative play. All of these terms refer to the same type of play, but I have chosen to refer to it simply as dramatic play. I can still remember how much of a part of my own childhood dramatic play was, and how endless the possibilities seemed as my friends and I collaborated on story lines, characters, and worlds. For me, this type of play continued through middle school as my friends and I would write and direct mini movies and record them on our Sony Video Camera.

Watching young children engage in dramatic play is so natural that we usually take it for granted, however, it reveals robust natural-born creativity that occurs without guidance or instruction. This is fascinating, for what these children are doing is quite complex! Most children begin engaging in dramatic play at around two-and-a-half-years-old and it usually lasts until the age of nine or ten (for me and my friends, more like thirteen or fourteen). In dramatic play, children explore concepts, ideas, and feelings that they have been exposed to as well as those they have imagined. There is a fundamental rule, either implicitly or explicitly communicated, that all players abide by a shared understanding of the roles each player is in. There is also shared understanding about what physical elements of the environment including props are imagined to be something else. Children do not forget who they really are and the reality of their environment, but they hold the imaginative ideas in their working memory and respond flexibly to the evolving storyline. They are taking on multiple perspectives, collaborating, creating meaning, iterating, and practicing cognitive flexibility.

But that is not all. As dramatic play encourages the imagination, it might be linked to another invaluable skill later in life, the ability to think counterfactually. To think counterfactually allows us to explore other perspectives as well as other possibilities and therefore to generate new hypotheses, ideas, and creations. It offers a safe space to practice the sophisticated mental skills involved in divergent thinking by temporarily adopting an alternate or potential reality, and considering its implications (Buchsbaum, et al, 2012). Plentiful research has found that children's imaginations and curiosity can be enhanced when dramatic play is encouraged as part of the curriculum or during recess (Kaufman, Singer, & Singer, 2013).

Dramatic play can be either free or mutually directed. Russian Psychologist, Lev Vygotsky, believed that of all activities, dramatic play gives children the greatest opportunity to become self-regulated and responsible. That is quite significant considering that the complex capacities that make up self-regulation are a crucial part of development and influence one's ability to learn and engage in the world. According to Vygotsky, in separating mental symbols from reality, children practice their internal capacity to regulate their actions as they incorporate the symbol to stand for a concept. Likewise, in engaging in rule-based play, they practice inhibitory control (impulse control) as they learn to act in socially desirable ways. Since Vygotsky's time, some studies have shown a positive correlation (though not a causal relationship) between dramatic play and self-regulation as well as other executive function skills. While the reliability, generalizability, and causal mechanisms are yet to be established, the investigation of such a relationship is worth our attention. Most adults do not realize the complex skills that could be developing in children through this age-old form of play.

An example of a school program with the aim of improving children's self-regulation skills through dramatic play is Tools of the Mind, developed by D. J. Leong and E. Badrova. Children make play plans before engaging in dramatic play, thereby practicing setting a goal, planning, and responding with cognitive flexibility and inhibitory control as they maintain their role. Creating play plans and similar practices are examples of how such play can be made an intentional part of curricula, but also shows how such play can be mutually directed. Teachers offer up support and scaffolding in the development of the plan, but let the children act as the agents of the play itself. After the play has occurred, teachers can further develop their executive function skills by inviting moments of metacognition (thinking about one's thinking). I frequently ask my students to reflect on what worked, what didn't work, and what they would do differently if they tried their play plan again.

Play and our social brain

Now let's look at the benefits of play to a child's burgeoning social skills. The majority of the play described above will include others in collaboration or partnership. As social beings we crave connection with others and need it for both proper brain development and the development of better social competence. Getting along with others, hearing others' ideas, and making agreements are amongst the most valuable of human survival skills, and these skills are practiced repeatedly in children's play.

Play and the Bayesian theory of learning

Reverend Thomas Bayes was an eighteenth-century theologian and a pioneer in probability theory. His probability theory has inspired one of the most influential accounts of human learning. The idea is that learning is much like scientific progress; we consider a range of possibilities or hypotheses, but none are absolutely sure to be true. When we say a hypothesis is correct, what we are really saying is that this is our best guess right now. New evidence would make us reconsider this best guess thus leading to our next best guess. This is also thought to be how we learn in general, and it can be seen in how young children play: they make observations, experiment, gather data, experiment some more, and on and on.

Building concepts and skills in literacy

Literacy skills can be incorporated into free, mutually directed, and guided play in a myriad of ways that could fill their own book. In all three main categories of play, children will naturally be exposed to vocabulary and will be intrinsically motivated to listen to understand and speak to be understood. Teachers that remain close by to document what is being said and how children are engaging in conversational play will be better equipped to take advantage of the children's momentum to extend and expand their oral language skills. Play is naturally a powerful tool for oral language development (that also leads to overall literacy development). An example of mutually directed play that supports literacy might be setting up a mail center with materials to invite children to write and deliver mail. Physical as well as teacher scaffolds will help the students remain intrinsically motivated, maintain agency, and learn. Subjects that could be taught this way include for example, writing conventions, how to form letters, how to sound out words or names, etc. Enacting plays or skits with simple scripts and labels for props is another example of mutually directed play designed to advance literacy skills. However, if more specific and discrete skills are being targeted, then guided play is a strong way to support literacy development. Any range of discrete literacy skills can be practiced through guided play. However, this suggestion to find creative ways to use play (free, mutually directed, and guided) is not meant to replace more direct reading programs – such as the formalized and systematic reading instruction programs run by some kindergartens or beginning from 1st grade.

Regardless of your school's philosophy around when to begin a more direct-instructional approach to reading, all preschool through kindergarten programs should be overflowing with exposure and practice of oral language, read-alouds, books, materials for writing, and phonological awareness. Phonological awareness is a game changer when it comes to the later skills that are necessary for *orthographic mapping*. Orthographic mapping is the gradual building of concepts or schema which connect letter-sound knowledge to spelling, pronunciation, and word meaning. This important foundational skill has consistently been shown to be a crucial element to learning how to decode (read) and encode (write) by science of reading research. Phonological awareness games are not a hard sell to young children either. Their brains are ready for this activity, and they are often entranced with rhymes in poems, songs, and stories. They are amused by games which invite them to isolate initial or final phonemes and get a kick out of correcting a silly teacher's mispronunciation. There are so many fun ways to manipulate sounds in words that the ideas are truly endless. I am continually amazed at how my students (both preschool and kindergarten) delight in singing nursery rhymes, switching up the cadence or the tune and keeping a beat. Repetitive exposure that allows for the discrimination between sounds and the creative manipulation of them seems to be consistently joyful.

Building concepts and skills in numeracy

Numeracy skills can also be incorporated into free, mutually directed, and guided play in many different ways. Children are born with certain mathematical understandings already pre-wired, such as approximate numerical quantities (Dehaene, 2011). As young children begin building their concepts of number symbols, the concept of *nominal* numbers usually precedes *ordinal* numbers and then *interval* numbers. Young children like to name and categorize as they make sense of their world. At the age of two or three, children will use number words without understanding them in a quantitative sense. By the age of three or four, many children have moved beyond simply understanding numbers in a nominal sense and now grasp the concept of ordinal numbers, that is that numbers can be put in an order and the position of one number is in respect to the position of another. This concept is greatly supported by engaging in sorting and ordination play such as with blocks or other size-graded toys that can be both grouped and ordered from smallest or shortest to biggest or tallest.

Similar, yet different to ordinal numbers, is the concept of cardinal numbers, which is the ability to count something (as opposed to indicating position in a series). Again, children often learn how to count before understanding the value relationship between numbers. Preschool children often learn *how* to count before they learn the *why*. However, once children grasp the *why* for counting, an outburst of numerical invention ensues. According to Stanislas Dehaene, 'Counting is the Swiss Army knife of arithmetic, the tool that children spontaneously put to all sorts of uses. With the help of counting, most children find ways of adding and subtracting numbers without requiring any explicit teaching' (2011). Once a child is able to use reason, often at the ages of five, six, or seven, they are able to construct interval numbers and arrive at a true understanding of units. This concept is significantly more complicated, for a true unit is at once both like and different from every other unit. To illustrate, the number seven is both like every other unit in that it is a number (its classification), however, it is also different from every other number in its order of enumeration (its ordination) and the value it holds. Seven has its own specific place on the number line and never comes before six or after eight. Whichever way one spreads out a group of seven objects, their number value does not change. Seven shells spread in a long line holds the same value as seven shells in a heap.

Only once a child has constructed the concept of interval numbers can they really engage in arithmetic operations. The unit concept is necessary to all quantification. One cannot measure or compare quantities without a concept of units. It is hard to overestimate the importance of giving children plenty of repeated hands-on practice with physical manipulatives (what Elkind calls mastery play) in attaining these different unit measurements. It is when a child experiments with classifying many different things, by color, size, pattern, and so on, that they develop the ability to classify. Likewise, only by ordering many different things according to size, or weight, or time, does a child hone their ordination skills. 'With this play experience the child is ready, when maturation kicks in, to coordinate the classification (cardinal) and the ordination (ordinal) into a true unit concept that can be added, subtracted, multiplied, and divided' (Elkind, 2007).

Seo and Ginsburg (2004) reviewed 15-minute video recordings of 90 four and five-year old children as they played. They were watching for what types of mathematics occurred naturally and spontaneously in unstructured, exploratory play. Six categories of mathematical content emerged:

- Classification (grouping or sorting by attribute).
- Magnitude (comparing the size of objects).
- Enumeration (counting, subitizing, or reading/writing numerals).
- Dynamics (putting things together and/or taking things apart).
- Patterns and shape.
- Spatial location (describing location or direction).

While this study is now almost 20 years old now, its findings illustrate a few pertinent points when it comes to math and play; 1) math is inherently interesting to children and emerges in their play with great frequency and range, 2) foundational concepts of math can be explored and practiced through free, mutually directed, and guided play, and 3) teachers can incorporate math goals in designing guided experiences.

One of the core knowledge areas that emerges in young children is their spatial abilities as they learn about their environment. This knowledge area includes being able to interpret a picture, understand maps, build and scale models, as well as make and interpret intentional lines that help us use symbols, especially in letters and numbers. These early abilities, when fostered, have been shown to enhance mathematical abilities in K-4th grades and this relationship starts as early as three years of age (Gagnier & Newcombe, 2021). Looking further down the road, high school students with good spatial skills tend to go into STEM fields and do well (e.g. Shea, Lubiniski & Benbow, 2001; Lubinski & Benbow, 2009). According to a study by Dillon, et al (2017), 'When five-year-old children practice these tasks [navigating maps and perceiving geometric structures] for four months, their spatial abilities are improved, not only when they are tested during the first three months that follow the practice, but also when they are tested a full year later, with no intervening opportunities for additional practice or rehearsal' (quoted in Spelke & Shutts, 2022). The connection to play is almost as boundless as play is itself. There are many good games that are specifically designed to use these skills such as Swish, Equilibrio, and Tangrams, to name just a few. But one does not need to go buy a product to foster spatial development skills in the classroom. If children are engaged in activities like observational drawing and block building, they are building their spatial reasoning. If they are working on puzzles, building with Legos, identifying and describing shapes (both 2D and 3D), or interpreting or making graphs and diagrams, then they are building spatial reasoning and simultaneously, spurring the development of important mathematical skills.

Building concepts and skills in science

One thing that I find most intriguing about young learners is their instinctive tendency to act like scientists and how much science is already part of children's play. Science begins with observation. It then tries to categorize or classify based on those careful observations. Building from there, it uses hypotheses and experimentation to create further understanding, which in turn leads to more observations, more hypotheses, and more experiments. Of course, this is to put it in simplistic terms, but children take a similar approach to how they seek to understand the world around them, from their very earliest days. It follows that intentionally introducing elements of science into a preschool and kindergarten program could not be more natural. As children have an innate talent and interest in observing, naming, and ordering plants, animals, and objects, we can encourage this in their play. Formal experimentation in which one holds some variables constant while varying others is best introduced when the children are older and developmentally better able to participate, but children do experiment all the time. Recently, a student of mine was waiting to use the bathroom. There is a school rule about how many people can be in the bathroom at one time. After waiting for some time, this child came up with an alternative plan. There was a teacher monitoring the bathroom so she couldn't just walk in. She theorized, however, that if she made her body less visible by sliding into the bathroom on the floor on her belly, the teacher would not notice. Alas, it didn't work, and she was duly escorted back to my classroom. I asked her what happened and she explained the situation and her thinking. I said to her, 'you had a theory that if you were not seen, you could enter the bathroom without anyone knowing. You hypothesized that if you slid on your belly, the teacher would not see you. Did your experiment work?' The child answered, 'no.' I responded, 'Well then, your experiment taught you something. Now, do you still need to use the bathroom?'

Do you recall the research linking spatial thinking and STEM in the previous section on mathematical skills? Well, naturally, those same forms of play and playful learning activities hold great promise for improving early understanding and skills in science in children (Gagnier & Fisher, 2020).

Developing executive function skills

Children in the early years of schooling are in the process of becoming self-regulators. As they grow older, their supporting brain structures continue to develop and, ideally, this is in tandem with opportunities to practice self-regulation and other executive function skills (Bunge, et al, 2002). While causal connections between play and executive functions are not definitive, many researchers believe that children can practice and strengthen executive function skills such as focused attention, inhibitory control, working memory, cognitive flexibility, and thoughtful decision-making through play (Shonkoff, et al, 2011). This set of skills manifest as the ability to follow directions, to take turns, to engage in prosocial problem-solving, to sustain attention on a challenging task, and to plan for future goals. When play happens within a group, its success relies on collaboration, which in turn relies on self-regulation or executive function skills. It would follow that providing ample time for children to play and collaborate provides the necessary practice they need to develop such complicated skills. Executive function skills also make possible the use of metacognition or reflection to inform future decisions. What do I mean by this? When children reflect on their play plan, its success or lack thereof, and decide to make changes, they are practicing a level of metacognition. If prompted by a teacher to verbalize their reflections after a period of play, children can see the connection between reflecting, iterating, and planning. While this is true in various forms of play, as a teacher, I see it most during dramatic play.

The challenge of assessing learning

The integration of the assessment of learning during play is a challenge for preschool and kindergarten teachers, both conceptually and practically. Whether teachers are using free, mutually directed, or guided play, the tools and strategies for what is observed and how to interpret those observations are going to matter. Having a set of goals is necessary for the design of play, as well as deciding how to scaffold or extend, knowing what to observe and document, and how to assess. If the goal of a free play session, for example, is to allow children to build social skills, enjoy themselves, and for the teacher to learn more about what the children find interesting, then the teacher(s) will rely heavily on written observations, but might also include video and photographs, which would then be analyzed and inform future projects and play opportunities. If, on the other hand, the goal for a guided play session was for children to practice specific academic skills, then observations recorded in a more structured format, such as a graphic organizer, would be helpful. In both examples, intentional time needs to be dedicated to the review, interpretation, and possible discussion with colleagues, of these observations to assess the learning and to consider next steps.

Dispositions of mind in early childhood

The styles and application of play we have been discussing are very much connected to a disposition of mind in young children! Young children are driven by a yearning to understand and to gain new skills. They have a knack for endless questioning and exploring. They use and develop intellectual curiosity, imagination, and creativity. During free, mutually directed, and guided play, children have agency, explore ideas, engage in creative processes, build social skills, make meaning, and gain knowledge.

Play as a pedagogical approach towards learning happens less in schools that feel a pressure to demonstrate academic excellence on standardized tests. However, the perception that teachers can *either* implement standards and accountability-driven instruction or allow children to play is a false dichotomy. This persistent false dichotomy between play and rigor inevitably impacts a child's disposition of mind towards learning and whether they see school as a place for them. More and more elementary aged children have been referred for counseling or mental health services in recent years and research suggests that age-appropriate playful learning may curb this distressing trend (Allee-Herdon, Taylor, & Roberts, 2019). This is not to say that a lack of play is the cause of poor mental health. However, I do want to emphasize that play has a protective quality against stress that helps children experience happiness while developing skills, passions, interests, and social connections – all of which are also positively correlated to health and well-being.

Summary

Children have an instinctive desire to play and this suggests that it serves not just one, but many, important functions. There is a direct connection between well-being and learning. Play, especially when intentionally incorporated into a program with a balance of free, mutually directed, and guided play has the power to enhance learning and well-being in mutually-reinforcing ways. The importance of play in early childhood is demonstrated in how it contributes to joy, social connection, and agency, and how it can be a protector against stress. It also aids the development of crucial self-regulation and executive function skills which can be applied to academic learning to build the foundations for later scholastic achievement. The value of play cannot be overstated. Play is imperative in the healthy development of young children's cognition, neural plasticity, readiness to work within social norms, setting and meeting learning goals, and developing an enduring and beneficial disposition of mind towards learning itself.

Invitation to inquiry

- How does play help children build neural networks and serve to both attract and retain their attention?

- How does free play differ from guided play in the way it is defined and experienced?

- What are the connections between play and the foundations for lifelong health?

- Increasing numbers of US children attend preschool and kindergarten programs that are narrowly focused on academic training, and this is especially true for low-SES families. Considering the promising relationship between self-regulation and play, should this be a cause for concern regarding equity?

Aligning with practice

- Listening is an invaluable teaching skill. Regardless of the type of playful learning that is occurring in the classroom (free, mutually directed, or guided), teachers need to listen carefully to what children are verbalizing. This is true whether these verbalizations are in the form of self-talk or in conversation with others; this allows teachers to scaffold at the right moments to extend learning.

- An important aspect to incorporate into a classroom that prioritizes play is a system of documentation. During free play, teachers are largely listening, observing, and jotting down information about the children's interests, creative and intellectual pursuits, social skills, and ways of conceptualizing. These notes help the teacher(s) make informed decisions about further scaffolding, inspirations for future projects, assessment of skills, and relationship building.

- Design learning spaces with intention and attention to detail to be interactive, investigative, and personalized to the interests of the children in that particular class. They should also be connected to prior learning. If we are to maintain such intentional design, then learning spaces should evolve as children's interests grow and change. This practice will also serve to add novelty and spark new or greater interest in the learning materials.

- Include student choice whenever possible and follow up with a reflection question, helping the children make connections between their choices, interests, and learning goals.

- Create a classroom routine in which children gather and share their ideas for play before heading out to recess. Through this practice, children practice setting goals, communicating those goals to peers, collaborating on a plan, monitoring the group's progress while in play, maintaining the cognitive flexibility necessary to maintain the role in that play, and lastly, reflecting on the success or lack thereof when they return from recess. Positive side effects to this practice include documentation of who children play with, what their play ideas were, as well as an increased awareness of their peer's creative and imaginative ideas. Other possible positive side effects could be an increase in creativity and a broadening of social relationships.

Further reading

Elkind, David (2007) *The Power of Play: Learning what comes naturally.*

Gray, Peter (2013) *Free to Learn: Why unleashing the instinct to play will make our children happier, more self-reliant, and better students for life.*

CHAPTER 8:
EMOTION AND COGNITION

Thanks to our intelligent, plastic brain, we can also develop emotions that color and steer our intellectual and social endeavors, such as curiosity to make us explore and discover, admiration to make us emulate the virtue of others and compassion, indignation, interest, and 'flow.'

Mihaly Csikszentmihalyi (1990)

What are emotions? They are the subjective behavioral and mental reactions we have to situations and concepts. They are immediate, automatic, and influence our bioregulatory response. Some are fleeting and some are enduring. Enduring emotions can be considered a mood. Different emotions propel us to act in different ways. We can think of emotions as both *drivers* and *shapers*. A *driver* because emotions play a role in our motivations. If we think of steering through life as like driving a car, then emotions are involved in our decision-making about the direction we take (steering wheel), what we approach (gas pedal), and what we avoid (the brake). Simultaneously, emotions are *shapers*. They shape our experiences and become embedded in them, in turn, driving future motivations. Emotions not only drive and shape experience and cognition, but also help to organize them. Relationships and emotional communications are the central organizing processes for the development of the brain (Immordino-Yang & Demasio, 2007; Siegel, 2020). Emotions and the role they play in our behaviors and experiences are incredibly complex.

Another way to think of the interconnectedness of emotion and cognition is by way of memory and attention. There is no new learning without memory and attention, and both of these are linked to emotion. Emotions provide the information our brains use to decide what is worth attending to. Likewise, the depth of an emotion will directly impact what is remembered. So, we cannot have a serious conversation about education without emphasizing the role played by emotions. Furthermore, another crucial and undeniable truth about emotions is that they are ever present! We are always feeling something ... and usually more than one thing at a time. Emotions are always flowing through us; stronger ones force us to pay attention to them while subtle ones feel like background noise. Whether we are a young student or a mature teacher, our days from the moment we wake up, through the school day, to when we fall back asleep are accompanied by a constant flow of feelings, feelings that impact current and future learning as well as well-being.

Why does a five or six-year-old learn how to read? There are multiple possible reasons: to attain the intrinsic reward of accomplishing a new skill; to become more independent and enjoy self-reading stories; to meet an expectation that has been given to them; to impress peers, siblings, teachers, and parents; and to become able to learn new information on their own. As Immoridino-Yang and Demasio discuss in their work, all of these reasons 'have a powerful emotional component and relate both to pleasurable sensations and to survival within our culture' (2007). What does this mean for educators? It means we cannot view emotion and cognition as two seperate aspects of learning and development. Emotions are not just by-products of the learning that happens in a classroom. They are directly related to cognitive performance, academic achievement, health, and career trajectories. In school and in the real world, cognition and emotion function in the service of each other to set and reach goals, to make wise decisions, and to succeed.

For the sake of simplifying a very complex concept, I have created a quick bullet pointed list. Emotions are central to our learning and growing experiences in school and beyond because emotions affect:

- What we pay attention to.
- What we remember.
- How we remember.
- Our decision-making processes.

- Our social relationships (including how we interpret others' actions).
- Our health (physiological and mental).
- Creativity and performance.

This is why I think that high quality teaching depends upon a deep understanding of the role emotions play in learning.

Biological functions of emotions

'[E]motions evolved and are present in all complex creatures because they are essential to managing life' (Immordino-Yang, 2016). They enable us to accomplish fundamental life tasks and are inextricably linked to both survival and thinking. Many of us have heard similar statements before and accept their veracity, but it is helpful to understand the implications more fully. Let's begin with the *biological functions* of emotions that are connected to survival. Firstly, emotions help us *react*, and secondly, they help us *regulate* internally in the face of those reactions. For example, if a situation is life threatening, our emotion will be fear, and this will dictate our reaction. Automatically, our bodies will be alerted to regulate blood flow differently, change our breathing and heart rate, and shut off some parts of our brain while engaging others – all for the sole purpose of surviving that moment. When our life is threatened, what we attend to in those milliseconds of the event can be a matter of life and death. We can, therefore, understand from a biological and physiological perspective, how emotions strongly influence our attention. This reaction helps us stay alive when the threat to our physical well-being is real (thank you, emotions!). However, at other times, when the level of threat is misinterpreted, misunderstood, or misguided, this reaction can be unhelpful. For example, regardless of whether the threat is an oncoming car or the fear of embarrassment during public speaking, our bodies have evolved to react and regulate quickly for the purpose of survival. In the first case this reaction might be helpful, but it in the second it will likely be actively unhelpful.

At some point in our lives, all of us have experienced a bodily sensation as a result of an emotion. It could be a boost of energy, a tummy ache, or a feeling in our skin. The complex relationships between emotion, bodily sensation, thinking, learning, and decision making are intertwined. Neuroscientist, Antonio Demasio, was able to show that typical subjects experience skin conductance responses even before they are even cognitively aware that they are entering a risky situation. Emotions trigger body responses as we think about a decision and its potential outcome just as it triggers bioregulatory processes in response to a current situation. Everyone has heard the phrase, 'just go with your gut.' Well, believe it or not, there might be some science to that. Your gut is connected by nerve endings to your brain and your gut might be detecting an emotion and a situation before you are able to process the words to describe or make sense of it.

Insights from affective neuroscience

I have separated the section on biological functions of emotions from the section on learning for the purposes of explanation, chunking, and to organize our thinking. However, no real separation exists (just as no real separation between cognition and emotion exists). Affective neuroscience (the neuroscience of emotion and cognition) tells us that the relationship between the biological functions of emotions and learning and thinking is best thought of as a web. This web of relationships between survival, bioregulatory response, and learning 'runs much deeper than many educators realize and is interwoven with the notion of learning itself' (Immordino-Yang, 2016). The experiential and neurobiological reality is that emotion and cognition are innately linked and cannot be separated. Affective neuroscience is a field that looks to understand the neural systems that regulate our survival, but that also regulate our sociocultural and intellectual lives. The insights born out of this field of study have enormous implications for pedagogy and education. 'Just as poets and artists have suspected for millennia, we feel social relationships and appreciate intellectual achievements using the same brain systems that sense and regulate our guts and viscera, adjust our blood chemistry and hormones, conjure our awareness and consciousness' (Immordino-Yang, 2016). As our brains evolved to optimize survival, emotions became increasingly part of that story and are therefore profoundly intertwined with our bodies and our minds. This evolution happened (and is still happening) alongside the development of human societies and our rich cultural and social heritage, a heritage that includes learning from one another.

In a school setting, an emotion can motivate us to further our understanding, take a risk, and narrow our attentional focus. Likewise, in a classroom or teachers' lounge where social relationships are an integral part of the experience, an emotion can motivate us to encourage one another, to share a laugh, or to offer assistance. But emotions do not have to be 'pleasant' to motivate learning and engagement. For example, the feeling of anger about an injustice can motivate a learner to attack a problem with focus, passion, and determination. Whether in a school setting or not, emotions, as a dimension of cognition, can motivate an individual to lead a movement, meet inspirational goals, or indeed shut down, or look for an escape route. And this brings us to the learner in the classroom.

Emotions of the learner

Our high-level cognitive skills, including reasoning, decision-making, problem-solving, reading, writing, and mathematics 'do not function as rational, disembodied systems, somehow influenced by but detached from emotion and the body' (Immordino-Yang & Demasio, 2007; Immordino-Yang & Fischer, 2008). The role emotions play in shaping our experience and our ability or inability to absorb and use new information in meaningful ways is profound. Recall that the amygdala, which sits at the center of the brain, is widely connected to other brain regions, and therefore, influences almost every system in the brain. This is true in a broad sense, but also in specific ways. For example, in studies looking at the brain, Immoridino-Yang (2015) has showed that the same brain systems involved in complex literacy tasks are involved in social emotional experiences. In concrete ways, we are now able to see how deeply intertwined emotions and learning are in the very way we perceive and experience the world.

All teachers are aware that emotions are essential to classroom experiences just as all teachers know that emotions impact learning. Younger children can be very expressive of their emotions, both pleasant and unpleasant, making their impact known. Other children, however, can be naturally more reserved. Whether the student emotes for all to see and hear or internalizes, those emotions influence *how* they learn, *if* they learn, and *what* they learn. Furthermore, how teachers and peers respond or react to a student's emotions (whether overtly expressed or not) also has a strong influence on learning. Learning in school, happens in classrooms with other people, and each person is influenced by both their own emotions and those of others.

A study by the late Alice Isen and her colleagues at Cornell University demonstrates the power of positive emotions for cognitive processes. In a controlled experiment, they showed one group of participants a comedy film while the other group didn't see any film. They were all then tested on creative thinking. As you might have guessed, there was a clear increase in creativity for the group of participants that watched the comedy film (Brackett, 2019). This is fascinating in and of itself of course, but it also speaks to the benefits of adding a sense of humor to our classes. Especially in moments when we are asking children to think deeply and creatively.

There is a psychological phenomenon in which we all have a natural bias to perceive and retrieve 'mood-congruent' information. Our mood – the effect of our emotions – influences what and how we perceive as well as what we do with these observations and experiences. When we are in more positive moods, we are more likely to see the positive in our experiences. Likewise, when we are in negative moods, we are more likely to interpret the same information or experiences in a more negative light. Taking the temperature of the room, and of the individual children, as best we can, gives us valuable information when making curricular and pedagogical decisions on the spot.

To illustrate how the bias for mood-congruent information affects even those with fully developed prefrontal cortexes, consider a study done at Yale. Teachers were divided into two groups. One group was asked to think and write about some of their positive classroom experiences while the other group was asked to recall a negative memory. Both groups were then asked to grade the same middle school essay. Of course, these teachers all strive to be objective and fair when grading, but what do you think happened? 'The positive-mood group marked the essay a full grade higher than the negative-mood group' (Brackett, 2019).

Sensing a less desirable mood in the classroom, a teacher might want to address this with a joke, a short and fun physical activity, or by giving children an additional free play break time. This is not only taking care of the children's well-being in the moment, but it can also help to prime them to get more out of the planned learning experience when you return to it. Mood boosting will be the appropriate strategy to use sometimes, but not always. Teachers know that sometimes giving children the permission and the space to feel the uncomfortable or unpleasant emotion is the best course of action. Crying can be beneficial as it carries stress hormones out of the body – no wonder children often feel better after a cry.

In early childhood, children are still developing expressive language skills as well as emotional intelligence, therefore, what is going on in the child's mind is not always apparent and can even be misleading. For this reason, teachers have to pay close attention to children's demeanor – their tone, facial expressions, and body language – for clues as to what their words and behavior mean, and what emotions might lie beneath them. This might be one of the hardest parts of our job, and some behaviors and emotions are easier to interpret than others. As is the case with many aspects of our pedagogy, documenting our observations and theories so that we can reflect and discuss them with colleagues, helps us make the best decisions in support of children's well-being and learning.

Emotions and relevance

The brain is a highly expensive metabolic tissue. That might seem like an odd and perhaps overly technical statement to put in a book about early childhood education, but bear with me. Because the brain requires more metabolic energy than other tissues and organs, efficiency is key. An individual only has so much energy and therefore what the brain attends to has to be worth the cost. Children's brains, like all human brains, are built to only think about things that actually matter to them. Teachers and parents will attest to the fact that children often think certain things matter that really don't in the grand scheme of things, but if the brain identifies relevance, then (and only then) it will attend. Without internally driven motivation from perceived relevance, memories are not likely to be stored and knowledge will not likely be usable. This is why teachers try to make their lessons relevant and meaningful to the children in their class. Because children often differ in what is meaningful to them, the teacher must know their students and try to find that hook for each individual student.

Teachers and scholars of education have long talked about the value of intrinsic motivation. As teachers in early childhood, we have a powerful advantage and that is the immense curiosity and creativity that most children walk in the door with. The intrinsic motivation for effortful learning is oftentimes already there. If we teach in a school that allows for flexibility in curriculum and schedules, then we can take advantage of those conditions to create deep learning experiences around the interests that children express. Relevance is built in when we are exploring a topic that interests us. This requires a lot of work on the part of the teacher, but it is a way of using children's emotions as drivers and shapers of rich learning.

Emotions associated with surprise or novelty and even confusion can also capture the attention of a learner and motivate them to discover more. This is another strategic way to use emotions as hooks to get children engaged and is something that should be designed into lesson plans. It won't always be possible, but if we are not intentionally inserting elements of surprise when we can, we are leaving out ways to stimulate curiosity and elevate the relevance of topics. Each time a child feels the excitement generated by a discovery that was supported by a teacher, we are helping them foster a healthy disposition of mind towards learning in school.

Emotions and emotional intelligence

Emotion regulation

Emotion creates our subjective experience and in so doing, how we experience life, our identity, and how we engage with others. Conceptualizing this is like the chicken and the egg problem, because emotional processes are 'both regulated and regulatory' (Siegel, 2022). Emotions help to create our understanding of 'self,' and the 'self' is what tries to regulate our emotions. While conceptually this is complicated and fascinating, the salient point here is that emotional intelligence, including emotional regulation skills, are a crucial part of how we achieve our goals while maintaining flexible, adaptive, and organized behavior.

Emotions, like cognition, have developmental pathways. This is why we speak of emotional intelligence as something that can be actively developed and attained. The skills that fall under the umbrella of emotional intelligence are complex and build upon one another. Many young children that we work with experience several emotions throughout the day that they don't understand. Oftentimes, they don't know what caused an emotion in the first place. Nor do they have the tools to regulate or control it. This lack of control, especially when it has such impact, is scary to the child. Foundational skills in emotional intelligence include the ability to recognize the emotion one is having, as well as to recognize emotions in others. To be able to recognize an emotion and give it a name gives the child that first little bit of control back: 'I know what this is. This is called frustration, and I have felt it before.' That is why recognizing and labeling emotions develop in tandem as children build 'emotion vocabulary.' The increasing vocabulary, coupled with an increasing conceptual understanding of what those words mean, helps them to organize their thoughts. Their growing vocabulary also allows them to communicate effectively with peers, teachers, and parents about those feelings. With explicit and intentional pedagogy and curricula, teachers can help children develop these skills so that they can then better understand their own emotions as well as emotions in others.

Eventually, children work on the most sophisticated skill under the umbrella, emotion regulation. Emotion regulation allows the child to acknowledge and name a feeling that arises, with both an awareness of how it is affecting them, and the ability to decide their response to it. This is a bidirectional interaction that is happening between their limbic system and prefrontal cortex, and it is hard for adults, let alone children with developing prefrontal cortexes. There are several good emotional intelligence curricula out there and I have not reviewed all of them, but I do want to highlight one in particular and that is the R.U.L.E.R. program developed at Yale's Center for Emotional Intelligence by Marc Brackett and colleagues. With the help of explicit teaching, experience, and maturity, children (and adults) can learn to respond instead of react, organize patterns of thoughts and behaviors, and adaptively accommodate emotional responses and experiences. Teachers of young children know that having emotional intelligence (and skills) is part of having a repertoire of cognitive and behavioral strategies and options for flexible and creative thinking, one of our chief aims in education.

Emotions and stress

No one is going to get through life without feeling strong and unpleasant emotions. However, the more we understand about why we are having them and the effect they have, the better we can regulate them productively. As a teacher of young children, we are also co-regulating these emotions with our students, that is, we are providing the scaffolds and tools to help them until they are able to regulate them on their own. Understanding what feelings like fear, anxiety, and anger do to one's ability to think is especially useful when observing and interpreting children's behavior.

Strong feelings affect all humans similarly, young and old, in that they narrow our minds. According to Marc Brackett (2019), 'it's as though our peripheral vision has been cut off because we're so focused on the peril that's front and center'. When gripped by an intense unpleasant emotion, we all struggle to see the whole picture and there is a neurocognitive reason for that. Recalling what we know about our limbic system, when we are experiencing strong emotions such as fear and anxiety, our brains secrete the stress hormone cortisol. This release inhibits the processing of information in our prefrontal cortex, the part of our brain that we recruit when considering information and outcomes and making informed decisions. Again, in the face of an imminent threat, we don't have time to consider multiple perspectives; survival means acting swiftly. This is why, in this situation, it is imperative to help validate the emotion of the child and help them calm down before trying to explain or teach. Once the child is calm then access to their prefrontal cortex has been restored. Providing the child with the opportunity to reflect afterwards can help them the next time they are experiencing that emotion. As early childhood educators are well aware, oftentimes unpleasant emotions occur due to a social conflict. In the same way, after calming down, the child should have the opportunity to repair a relationship that may have been damaged with the support and scaffolding of the teacher. Empathy is one of the more important skills that we want children to acquire. Modeling empathy for students and their emotional states has the power to teach empathy while simultaneously, co-regulating the emotion, strengthening the teacher/student relationship, and helping them grow from the experience.

Just as not all unpleasant emotions can be avoided, not all stress is bad. Moderate levels of stress releases adrenaline and norepinephrine which heighten our perceptions and motivation therefore enhancing learning. The problem is when stress is extreme and chronic. In these cases, elevated stress hormones can significantly damage limbic components such as the hippocampus, anterior cingulate gyrus, and amygdala. High or chronic stress also depresses the immune system, tenses the muscles, and creates social/emotional barriers. According to stress physiologists, the area of the brain most affected by early and chronic stress is the prefrontal cortex. Children who have experienced chronic stress will find it harder to concentrate and absorb information, harder to regulate their response to disappointment, and harder to follow directions. Understanding that chronic stress might be behind a child's undesirable behaviors helps us to help them. Again, this is why we co-regulate in the moment and intentionally design curricula to help children develop emotion regulation skills. This is also why we put so much effort into building relationships of trust and care and why we should create classroom environments and activities that counteract stress.

The emotions of the teacher

Teachers' emotions matter too. They matter a lot. Our emotions don't just matter because they impact the children (although they do), they matter because everyone's feelings matter. Period. It is all too common for teachers to sacrifice their own well-being for the sake of others or some expectation that has been communicated either intentionally or unintentionally by society or the school administration. Not only is this inhumane, but it also simply doesn't work and is not sustainable. If our beliefs and values are to be aligned with our actions, then we – administrators, parents, and members of society, and teachers themselves – need to treat teachers as well as we treat children. If we are to model a caring world, children should see this demonstrated in how teachers are cared for as well. If we want to elevate the value teachers have in our society, we cannot do that while disregarding their emotions. I will elaborate on this topic more in the chapter thirteen on creating a culture of care, but I had to open with it here before jumping into the other crucial aspect of the emotions of the teacher: how they impact the emotions of the learner.

> No one cares how much you know until they know how much you care.
>
> attributed to Theodore Roosevelt

Just as a teacher's anxiety or lack of enthusiasm while teaching will have an effect on students, so will their expressed excitement or passion. Studies have connected teachers' enjoyment of teaching to their student's enjoyment of learning (Frenzel, et al, 2018). Most early childhood teachers became teachers because they love to be around children, to help them, foster a love of learning, teach them knowledge and skills, and help them thrive in life. These motivations are tied to our own enjoyment while teaching and are felt by children through our warmth, patience, and enthusiasm. When it comes to content and skills building, teachers can also look for ways to incorporate aspects that are particularly interesting or fascinating to them. If you have not been enjoying a unit of study or project yourself, ask yourself what you can do to infuse more joy for yourself. Chances are this is a way to also increase the children's happiness and joy and therefore, their motivation for the learning experience.

Emotions and motivation

It would be wrong to say that all pleasant emotions help learning and all unpleasant emotions hinder learning. Pleasant emotions such as excitement can hinder learning, for example if the excitement is for something other than the learning experience. Emotions that we typically think of as negative, such as 'anger', can help learning when recruited to help the child argue a case for social justice. Likewise, a little bit of stress when tinkering with a material or problem can have a beneficial motivational effect, as long as it is not overwhelming or chronic. This is why we need to be careful to not insinuate that schools should only be about increasing 'positive' emotions and decreasing 'negative' emotions. That is just a wild over-simplification that can lead to more harm than good.

There is another way to think of the importance of emotions in learning and that is through their relationship with motivation and disposition of mind. Psychological theories on motivation provide explanations for human drive. At school, and throughout life, individuals are called upon to interact with the world as well as others in it and will meet various obstacles along the way. Motivation theories help to explain the underlying mechanisms that support the human drive to develop skills and knowledge to engage, learn, and grow. Self-determination theory asserts that there are three basic psychological needs that must be met for optimal human functioning: autonomy, competence, and relatedness (Ryan & Deci, 2017). For autonomy, students need to feel like they have a say in how they think, act, and feel and that those choices reflect their genuine wishes. Students also need to have a sense of competence: that they have the capacity to engage, learn, interact, and contribute. The need for relatedness is reflected in a student's experience of positive and reciprocal relationships with teachers and peers. When students feel autonomy, competence, and relatedness, they are primed to meet challenges with success, and feel motivated autonomously. The concept of autonomous motivation is very much connected to identity formation and disposition of mind, for it relies upon an inherent interest, enjoyment, and recognition of the importance of learning.

Summary

As long as there are bodies and brains in the classroom, there are also emotions. As discussed, the role emotions play in our learning and behavior is incredibly complex and interconnected. Our emotions help us steer the direction we take, what we approach, and what we avoid. They not only shape our subjective experiences, but become embedded in those experiences, in turn driving our future motivations. Emotions not only drive and shape experience and cognition, but they also help to organize them. There is a direct link from emotion to motivation, memory, and attention and these are necessary ingredients for learning to happen in the brain. The neurobiological relationship between emotions and cognition can either help or hinder learning. Understanding this dynamic has the power to make a significant impact on how we learn and teach, how we see ourselves as learners and teachers, and where we go from here.

Aligning with practice

- Those in the field of education often talk about how we want children to behave or perform but rarely how we want children to feel. In the planning of lessons and curriculum, try adding a column to your physical or mental graphic organizer entitled, how do we want this activity/lesson to help children feel?

- As part of your daily practice, incorporate a 'welcoming station' in which children have a short check-in that is one-to-one with the teacher. Use these brief but daily moments as an opportunity to introduce and practice using a more sophisticated emotion vocabulary. Different tools can help in this regard such as feeling wheels, charts, or the Yale Center for Emotional Intelligence's Mood Meter (R.U.L.E.R. program).

- Provide ample opportunity for children to discuss the feelings of characters in books, plays, and skits and how the feelings are influencing the characters' actions.

- Validate all feelings of the students as this practice alone has the power to calm children down who are experiencing emotional intensity and discomfort. This will also help to build relationships.

- Prioritize the development of emotion regulation strategies such as deep breaths, taking short walks, or retreating to a 'safe space' in the classroom to calm children who have reached an intensity of emotion that has put them in reactive as opposed to a responsive state.

- Use humor to enliven the room and increase the release of hormones that aid in learning and engagement.

- Use metacognitive prompting when a child is calm to empower them to make better choices in the future. Help them generate alternative responses by asking questions such as, 'Is there another way that you could have responded?' 'How might a different response help you feel better should this happen again?'

- Since research has shown that a committed relationship to a trusted adult is the single most important factor in how children respond to stressors, find ways to make trust and personalized responsiveness to students part of your curriculum and practice.

Further reading

Immordino-Yang, Mary Helen (2016) *Emotions, Learning, and the Brain: Exploring the educational implications of affective neuroscience.*

Brackett, Marc (2019) *Permission To Feel: The power of emotional intelligence to achieve well-being and success.*

CHAPTER 9:
OUR SOCIAL BRAIN AS A NATURAL INCUBATOR FOR LEARNING

I believe that the individual who is to be educated is a social individual, and that society is an organic union of individuals. If we eliminate the social factor from the child we are left only with an abstraction; if we eliminate the individual factor from society, we are left only with an inert and lifeless mass.

John Dewey (1897)

When we survey our lives and endeavors we soon observe that almost the whole of our actions and desires are bound up with the existence of other human beings. We see that our whole nature resembles that of the social animals. We eat food that others have grown, wear clothes that others have made, live in houses that others have built. The greater part of our knowledge and beliefs has been communicated to us by other people through the medium of a language which others have created. Without language our mental capacities would be poor indeed, comparable to those of the higher animals; we have, therefore, to admit that we owe our principal advantage over the beasts to the fact of living in human society.

Albert Einstein (1934)

Healthy brain development requires social relationships. When given adequate opportunity to engage with others through supportive relationships with family members, teachers, and peers, children will grow, and develop an understanding of the world and how they fit into it. Engagement in social experiences contributes to patterns of thoughts and feelings. These patterns organize brain development over time and in age-specific ways thus influencing future growth and well-being.

Humans' amazing intellectual potential is connected to the way we have evolved to be social and to learn socially. It is our sociability that is behind the rapid spread of new knowledge and ideas (this was true even before social media). Indeed, all of our impressive cognitive achievements as a species, whether they be linguistic, mathematical, technological, artistic, or institutional, were made possible through the collaboration of many minds as opposed to the workings of just one. Even when working independently on a project, we are influenced and informed by relationships we have, words we have heard, books we have read, and the generations of thinkers and doers that came before us.

Harkening back to chapter four (Early Childhood from an Anthropological Lens) the story of humanity is one of reinvention and socialization and it begins when we are young. Individuals who have been motivated to support one another and engage in collaborative problem-solving are at an adaptive advantage. Our capacity to adapt to an ever-changing world relies on 1) our ability to learn and 2) our ability to form trusted relationships. This was true in the past. It is true today. We have reason to believe this will continue to be true in the future. To learn and to form trusted relationships are two interdependent and interconnected abilities that define a healthy childhood and a happy life. Since most learning is socially guided or happens within a social context, why wouldn't this be a major area for teacher/researchers to pay attention to? I considered omitting this chapter, when I became worried this book might be getting too long, but it is just not possible to talk about learning in school without spending time talking about our social brains.

Social neuroscience

Anthropology, psychology, and biology all concur that we are fundamentally social creatures that have depended on our emotions and ability to connect to others for survival throughout history. The recognition of the centrality of our social brains to our life experiences has resulted in the specialized field of social neuroscience. Social neuroscience looks at the brain's function in relating to other humans, for example, in communication, social perception, empathy, cooperation, social learning, social networks, cultures, etc. (Joldersma & Van Herwegen, 2022). Through the social neuroscience lens, researchers seek understanding of learning in social contexts or how the brain is shaped by social interactions and learning experiences with others. Taking the role of culture into account, social neuroscience also considers how cultural variation across the globe (and in our very own classrooms) might influence brain functioning leading to variations in how people think and act.

A guiding principle within social neuroscience is that the structure and function of the developing brain is greatly impacted by interpersonal relationships. These relationships can shape the genetically programmed maturation of the nervous system (see epigenetics, chapter six). For young children, patterns of warm, responsive, and respectful communication with adults, help shape the developing brain towards integration. What does that mean? When brain functions are integrated, children are better able to behave flexibly thus promoting healthy self-regulation (Siegel, 2022).

Social neuroscience thus gives us yet another reason to centralize relationships in how we design curriculum, teaching practice, and our environment. Incorporating daily routines that strengthen and support relationships between students and teachers and peers to peers will contribute to their learning, well-being, and overall development. I begin each class period in my science classes with a short game designed precisely for this purpose. Before I begin the lesson, I want the children to feel connected to the people in the room.

Making friends at school

At around the age of three, children begin to acquire social-cognitive skills that help them develop mutually rewarding relationships with other children. While many three year-olds have already begun forming relationships with siblings and peers, their focus will have been towards their caretakers. After the age of three, however, children begin to desire more social connection and play mates. They begin to have an awareness of the impression they are making on others and want to self-monitor their behavior. This is a type of self-regulation that develops with practice and over time. According to Tomasello (2019), 'By engaging in such social and cultural self-regulation from three to six years of age, young children come to create the many and various kinds of self-reflective, normatively structured, and reason-based forms of thought and action that make them for the first time reasonable and responsible persons.' The level of social cognition that allows small children to collaborate in the classroom or on the playground can eventually grow into the level of social cognition that promotes cultural achievements in the sciences and arts in adulthood. However, these skills come into being 'through a development process, extended over time, in which maturation, experience, and executive self-regulation [executive functions and emotion regulation] all play constitutive roles' (Waldinger & Schulz, 2023). Learning to make and maintain friendships is a central skill related to overall achievement and happiness in life. Learning to make friends at school is one of the best gifts that schooling can provide a developing child.

Much of what early childhood educators do in the classroom is connected to this goal of helping children develop social-cognitive skills and make and maintain friendships. Teachers are already reading books that highlight the values and skills involved with friendship. Many are already facilitating social conflict resolution between peers and explicitly teaching the skills of empathy and communication. Likewise, many of the learning experiences in early childhood classrooms involve group work and play. This is because whether they are aware of social neuroscience or not, teachers know the importance of these skills and experiences for children to learn and thrive.

Where emotions and social processing converge

External stimuli enter the brain via the sensory system and are quickly appraised by the amygdala (see chapter three on the amygdala and the limbic system). The amygdala reacts to questions like: is this something to pay attention to? Is it safe? Based upon this initial appraisal, the information can be sent for further evaluation to the anterior cingulate and orbitofrontal cortex. Eventually, the information is passed to the hippocampus (one of our memory structures) and to the prefrontal cortex (higher cognitive skills) for further appraisal and processing. As the brain is embodied, all of these processes also influence the body's physiological response.

The amygdala and other limbic systems are key agents in coordinating emotional and social input, but it is the communication with the prefrontal cortex that results in social cognition: how we interpret, respond, and remember (see chapter eight on emotion and cognition). All of these brain structures process incoming sensory data along with social context, that is, our brains are processing and making evaluative decisions based on information like facial expressions, directions of eye gaze, gestures, as well as other verbal and nonverbal social cues.

Emotions and social functioning are connected and contribute to the development of empathy and mindsight (the ability to take on another's perspective). Being able to perceive others' intentions and feelings helps us evaluate events, understand social interactions, anticipate behaviors, and form social bonds. If you have high emotional intelligence, you likely have high social intelligence as well, and these can be determining factors in finding success and happiness within human cultures and societies.

Social relationships, memory, and self

> The mind creates and is created by interactions with other minds.
>
> Daniel Siegel (2020)

Our social relationships influence brain development and the expression of our genes (see epigenetics, chapter six). This is just another way of saying that individuals co-regulate each other's physiology. The quality of a person's relationships with others shapes their development and the health of both their body and brain (Immordino-Yang, Hammond, & Krone, 2018). The way individuals experience social relationships in the home, community, school, or work, influences their biological development as well as how they think and experience the world.

Development of the frontal cortical regions of the brain is connected to autobiographical or episodic memory (memory of the self over time). This area of the brain begins to develop early but is continuously changing into adulthood. Young children and their caregivers together weave mutually constructed tales about the 'self'. Put another way, according to Siegel (2020), 'The richness of self-knowledge and autobiographical narratives appears to be mediated by the interpersonal dialogues in which caregivers co-construct narrative.' During the preschool years, children are slowly gaining a social-cultural-linguistic narrative of the self in society. This narrative is accompanied by a new awareness as well as changes in behavior. A longitudinal study by Jack and colleagues supports their hypothesis that 'past-event conversations during early childhood have long lasting effects on autobiographical memory' (Jack, et al, 2009). Children can be encouraged to see themselves as active learners with agency, intellectual curiosity, and creative contributions. As teachers – knowing that the narrative of 'self' continues to emerge in ever-enriching ways – we can help co-construct children's self-narrative to optimize for their sense of self-efficacy, purpose, and disposition of mind.

Social interactions and language

Children are wired to learn from *interactions with* and *observations of* others. It follows that much of learning is modulated by language. From an evolutionary, historical, and individual developmental perspective, we owe much of our intelligence to language that is exchanged between people whether it be oral or written. The power of language is clear when one really stops to think about the amount of information that is exchanged in the everyday conversations that we take for granted. Oral language is what our brains are hard-wired for and how it all begins. Young children typically learn oral language(s) at an impressive speed of which adults are envious. Children are adept at learning language through interactions and observations and the implications of this for education are clear. Children should be constantly exposed to social exchanges involving hearing and participating in oral language. According to an analysis done by Wang, et al (2020), children's vocabulary can be predicted by the number of conversational exchanges children participate in. Conversations are an under-utilized but important pedagogical tool in early childhood education. I have dedicated the following chapter to the topic.

Collaboration and cooperation

The idea that collaboration is important in education is not new. Lev Vygostsky, the Russian development scientist and theorist, asserted that collaborative learning is necessary in childhood education as meaning itself is socially constructed. Collaboration is a core skill necessary for social competence as a child and as an adult. When children are working collaboratively, they are more likely to get engrossed in the challenge of learning and less likely to focus on praise or product. It is also possible that collaboration helps children to internalize knowledge, in other words, to broaden and deepen their own schemata or understanding (Ostroff, 2012).

Trust

Trust looks different with different students, and is affected by factors like age, culture, background of experience, etc. Gaining the trust of a teenager who already has developed ideas of teachers and schools based on their previous experiences is going to be quite different to building trust with a young child. However, trust is important. The level of motivation for any task a student feels will be informed by how far they trust their teacher.

Social skill curriculum

Humans may be born to be social, but that does not mean we are born with social skills. As early childhood educators, we already know a thing or two about social emotional learning (SEL). We also know a thing or two about how children's feelings and social conflicts can instantly thwart our lesson or plan for the day. We have witnessed on countless occasions how emotions from some students can create a cascade of emotions in others. Yes, we know all about social-cognitive skills.

As children get older and mature, their emotion regulation develops, as does their understanding of social norms and conflict resolution. However, the work is not done there. During life's different stages, children need to be reminded of some of the basic social-cognitive skills that they were taught when they were young. Older children need opportunities to revisit those lessons in the context of their new age group and context. We all need to keep educating ourselves, reflecting on our social-cognitive skills, their importance, and their ubiquitous effect on us throughout our lives.

The question then becomes: how do we establish the conditions in early childhood that set our students up for a deeper understanding of their social relationships now and in the future? These skills need to be explicitly taught and revisited often. But if we want children to walk away with more than just a memorized list of good manners, we need to teach them a little bit about our social brains. And this needs to be taught in a way that increases meaning-making, purpose, agency, and retention. Therefore, we need to apply concepts of MBE.

Children of all ages (like all humans) want to maximize their social reward and minimize their social pain. We can use these two powerful motivations to increase children's social-cognitive skills. Beyond knowing what feelings are and how to act with others, we want to help them understand how and why our feelings and our relationships with others impact learning and happiness. Naturally, this will look quite different with toddlers, than four, five, or six-year-olds. Beginning with lessons or class discussions that establish a basic understanding of the importance of relationships in the classroom, we can begin explicitly building skills like perspective-taking, overcoming disadvantageous impulses, emotion regulation, cooperation, and empathy. Regardless of whether you are using a SEL program or creating your own, having clear goals and the time to revisit them in light of what is happening in the classroom is essential. As Matthew Lieberman (2013) says, by focusing on instilling these skills in school, 'we have an opportunity to craft far more socially savvy adults'. Imagine a world in which all adults you encountered had strong social-cognitive skills. That is definitely something we should be working towards!

Building strong social-cognitive skills starts with focusing on the relationships that the children have with peers, teachers, family members, and caretakers. Collaborative learning among peers is more likely to be successful when children are interested in the topic and have been given explicit frameworks for mutual respect. Once we have their attention with an interesting topic or activity, we can sustain it by making sure the students have agency and are making emotional connections through inquiry. Our goal is for children to build neural networks and to connect prior and new knowledge, aligned to this we can use inquiry and small or large group discussions to help them do some deep thinking, draw from their own experiences and connect to others. Dedicating a regular time in our day or week – such as a weekly 'Town Hall Meeting' – to talk about their social lives in the classroom communicates to the children that the teachers and the school value their social well-being as well as the development of their social-cognitive skills. It also increases vocabulary and gives the children practice in thinking and expressing thoughts on this topic. The only caveat to such meetings is that it is imperative that they are conducted in such a way as to not shame or embarrass anyone for making a social mistake. Just as important is to provide activities that give them opportunities to express their thoughts and ideas about their social world in different media. Their basic understanding will become more sophisticated as skills and experiences connect to one another. Their developing social-cognitive skills and increased knowledge will become self-reinforcing.

Summary

Humans are born with a powerful drive to be social. This drive has deep evolutionary biological roots. The fact that social and physical pain both use the same neural machinery illustrates how important social connection is to our survival and quest for happy lives. Knowledge of how our sociability acts as a natural incubator for learning creates opportunities for teachers to approach and design lessons differently. Social neuroscience has implications for the teaching of social-cognitive skills. However, we should be educating children about the centrality of these skills to their success in all areas of school and life.

Alignment to Practice

- What we make time for in our schedule communicates what we value. Many educators believe that social-cognitive skills are essential and say that they are incorporated into the 'everyday.' Yet, if we want to be truly intentional and effective, they should have a designated time in the day or week as well. This change, in and of itself, will have impact on your students' development of social-cognitive skills and knowledge.

- What we assess also communicates what we value. Provide children with opportunities for reflection and, depending on their age, self-evaluations on their own social-cognitive skills.

- As with all content areas, providing children with ample opportunities to express themselves in different media allows for agency, creativity, and meaning-making that makes the content more enjoyable and more impactful.

- It can be easier for children to engage with feelings and social conflict resolution when it is one step removed. Having children discuss characters in social situations from books or acting out short skits and then discussing them can be both engaging and fruitful in getting them to think deeply.

Further reading

Lieberman, Mathew, S. (2013) *Social: Why our brain are wired to connect.*

Siegel, Daniel J. (2020) *The Developing Mind: How relationships and the brain interact to shape who we are.*

Tomasello, Michael (2019) *Becoming Human: A theory of ontogeny.*

CHAPTER 10:
CLASSROOM CONVERSATIONS

Conversation is a living thing. It cannot be scripted in advance.

Ann Lewin-Benham (2011)

If I had to characterize the key difference between a high-quality and a low-quality preschool environment, it is this: in a high-quality program, adults are building relationships with children and paying a lot of attention to children's thinking processes and, by extension, their communication. They attend carefully to children's language and find ways to make them think out loud.

Erika Christakis (2016)

Relationships are at the heart of high-quality education. It follows that having frequent meaningful conversations with children is essential. Whether they are whole group, small group, or one-on-one, meaningful conversations provide the give and take moments that both inform our teaching practice in myriad ways, and also develop essential skills in children.

What is a conversation? Conversation is an extended exchange of thoughts and ideas related to a topic or set of topics between two or more participants. 'Meaningful conversations' meet these criteria, but additionally, the participants also feel a sense of agency and belonging through a shared intention of respect and meaning making. Meaningful classroom conversations hold space for each student to express themself. As meaningful classroom conversations become more artful, and the skills of the participants more advanced, they have the power to extend thinking routines and collaborative learning in powerful ways.

There are times in the school day that can be dedicated to organic conversations or teacher prompts while in small or large group conversation. As both a homeroom teacher and a science teacher, I like to create time at the start of class for a short game followed by an opportunity for children to share thoughts, ideas, and wonderings before delving into the lesson or instructions for the activity. I learn a lot about the children this way and they learn a lot about each other. Some of this information is used in the design of future lessons and projects. During lessons, however, I also create opportunities for children to converse in groups and practice the skills of speaking and listening. One way I do this is by introducing the word 'theory', and then using it repeatedly in sentences like, 'My theory about why _____ is _____ . What is your theory?' This simple practice invites thinking aloud and promotes the idea of learning communities while giving children practice with important conversational skills. Even our youngest learners gain skills by connecting their thoughts to the thoughts of others.

In addition to elevating the teacher's understanding of the needs, interests, and thoughts of their students (a good reason on its own), incorporating regular conversations into one's pedagogy and curriculum has the power to promote:

- Shared meaning and the broadening of perspectives.
- Supportive learning communities that encourage children's inquiry, agency, trust, and a sense of belonging,
- Children's ability to organize their thinking.
- Shared and sustained focus.
- Self-regulation.
- Intellectual curiosity and disposition of mind.
- The development of spoken language skills including:

  - Expressive oral language skills (communicating effectively).
  - Receptive oral language skills (listening and understanding).
  - Vocabulary and reading comprehension.

- Disposition of mind for intellectual curiosity.

Shared meaning and the broadening of perspectives

Classroom conversations link us to each other and to the world around us. It is when we are speaking and listening in a conversational exchange that we create shared meaning and broaden our perspectives. This is even the case if we come to understand that we simply disagree with another's perspective (and that is ok too). It is hard to gain understanding of another's perspective if one never hears it. Likewise, it is a challenge to take a second look at an assumption you have made if it has never been pointed out to you. This can be said for adult conversations as well as those between very young children – though the two naturally look different from one another. Regular classroom conversations have the power to instill a habit of listening to others and considering your own ideas in a new light. This will happen on different levels according to the age and stage of the participants. Children learn from other children, teachers learn from children, and children learn from teachers. Teaching and learning become reciprocal and everyone's knowledge is enriched in the process.

Supportive learning communities and a culture of belonging

Regular classroom conversations promote supportive learning communities by encouraging inquiry, agency, and trust. Trust grows through these conversations as children experience their voices being valued and teachers and peers listening to them. When done well and with intention, classroom conversations provide powerful opportunities to both implicitly and explicitly teach respect for diverse perspectives and opinions. Authentic collaborations are made possible as children exchange common interests and ideas. Over time, regular conversations and collaborations create opportunities for individual children to build social-cognitive skills while simultaneously building supportive learning communities. This is the point that I believe holds incredible power so I will repeat it again in a different way; while conversations help each individual child learn and gain important skills, they simultaneously connect each child and teacher together through the exchange of ideas, knowledge, perspectives, feelings, opinions, and wonderings. The key is honoring the voice of each member while knitting those voices together into the fabric of a learning community.

Many classrooms recognize the importance of having a morning meeting in early childhood classrooms, but the way these conversations go can vary drastically. In *Bringing Reggio Emilia Home* (1997), Louise Cadwell, describes a morning meeting that she witnessed at the Diana School in Reggio Emilia: 'Children and teachers chat, catch up, and share the pleasure of each other's company. There isn't any rush, there isn't a feeling that there is a need for control on the teacher's part. It is just pleasure.' The conversation flowed organically and children's ideas and projects from the previous days were discussed. Towards the end of the conversation, the teacher proposed ways to extend those projects and interests. This example reflects many similar morning meetings that I also had in some of the schools that I have taught. However, many morning meetings in US classrooms are rushed (if they happen at all), and many follow a specific format that is controlled by the teacher with little to no opportunity for variation. Many of those formats were created with great intentions and are informed by child psychology and sociology, for example, the practice of saying each child's name in the form of a daily greeting. This is grounded in good science as having each child hear their name during a morning meeting increases their sense of belonging. Young children also like the predictability that comes with routines. However, we can adopt these ideas and routines into our morning meetings *and also* allow for conversation that is not pre-planned and controlled by the teacher. Otherwise, we are missing out on enormous opportunities. The morning meeting conversation that Cadwell describes shows what is possible with young children: a supportive learning community, where children have a sense of belonging, and have acquired a high degree of language, listening, and collaborative thinking skills while fostering relationships and dispositions of mind.

Conversations help children to organize their thinking

Conversations prepare children to think logically as the exchange of ideas motivates them to understand and to be understood. When conversations are orchestrated by the teacher as a retelling of a shared learning experience, children are also learning how to organize their thinking and the sequence of events. In this way, conversations aid in memory and the child's ability to connect past learning experiences with current ones. Conversations help children connect their ideas to the ideas of others, and their perspective to the perspectives of others.

Conversation invites reflection and metacognition. When teachers use active reflection during conversation, they are helping children build memory and focus, and in turn, this helps children tell the story of their own learning. Meanwhile, encouraging children to reflect helps to develop meta-cognitive abilities, one of the educational interventions most highly linked to educational gains as demonstrated by John Hattie's meta-analyses (2009, 2012).

Conversations promote sustained shared thinking

Sustained shared thinking – sometimes referred to as 'episodes of joint attention' – is when children are invited to 'put their heads together' and verbally share thoughts and ideas about a particular topic. For example, engaging the class with what they think and notice about a particular image, or asking for impressions and questions after a shared experience. It can happen through whole class, large group, or small group conversations. Unfortunately, some believe that such conversations are not possible for younger children, but like most things, skills improve with practice with shorter activities preceding longer ones. An interesting study out of the United Kingdom demonstrated that frequent episodes of sustained shared thinking between adults and children during preschool was positively correlated with enhanced intellectual and personal gains, even overriding social disadvantage. These gains persisted throughout the 12 years of the study, culminating in enhanced results on national examinations when the children were 15 years old (Sylva, et al, 2004).

Conversations and self-regulation

Over time, as you use conversations in the classroom, the interchange of ideas will grow in length and sophistication, and this is a great sign of self-regulation amongst the students. Learning how to listen requires the use of inhibitory control (blocking out distractions and not interrupting), a key executive function skill that contributes to enhanced self-regulation. Responding to a peer's comment or a teacher's question also activates working memory as the child considers what has been said while formulating their response. Meanwhile, partners in conversation maintain their joint attention as the conversation moves along. In other words, the children have to re-align their goals and attention. These are definitely higher order thinking skills, and it has amazed me to watch children develop them over the course of a single school year whether it be in preschool or kindergarten.

Conversations and the development of spoken language

Spoken language is experience-expectant

Spoken language is 'experience-expectant'. What does that mean and why is it relevant? As a result of millions of years of evolution, the brain expects to have the experience of spoken language and is hardwired to do so efficiently. Unless the brain is seriously deprived of hearing language, it will develop this skill. Even though spoken language is experience-expectant, that does not mean that learning a language is simple. Jenny Saffran (2003), explains it this way:

> Imagine you are faced with the following challenge: You must discover the underlying structure of an immense system that contains tens of thousands of pieces, all generated by combining a small set of elements in various ways. These pieces, in turn, can be combined in an infinite number of ways, although only a subset of these combinations is actually correct. However, the subset that is correct is itself infinite. Somehow you must rapidly figure out the structure of this system so that you use it appropriately early in your childhood.

So, yes, oral language is experience-expectant and we are hard-wired to become increasingly more skilled in our abilities to speak and listen, but the level of sophistication we develop will still depend upon the amount and type of exposure and practice we have access to.

Expressive and receptive oral language skills

Literacy has always been a focus in schools and for good reason. Many people think of literacy as synonymous with reading and writing. However, it also includes speaking and listening, and these are not only precursors to reading and writing, but essential skills in and of themselves. These skills remain vital throughout one's life in school and beyond. However, before I elaborate on the skills of listening and speaking, let's explore the relationship between spoken language and reading and writing a little more.

One way to illustrate the relationship of listening and speaking to reading is the theory 'The Simple View of Reading' (Gough & Tunmer, 1986), a foundational concept in the science of reading.

$$D \times LC = RC$$

Decoding (Word Recognition) x Language Comprehension = Reading Comprehension

Decoding (or word recognition) is the child's ability to lift a word off of the page and involves many complicated skills in and of itself. Decoding is experience-dependent so it requires explicit instruction and a strong foundation in phonological awareness and phonics in order for children to build orthographic mapping in their brains. Children literally need to build neural networks that were not there before through repetitive practice. Decoding with fluency and automaticity strengthens reading comprehension. However, decoding is only half of the equation for reading comprehension. The other half is language comprehension and this is why children need frequent exposure to rich oral language in the forms of conversations, read-alouds, and eventually lessons on morphology in order to build vocabulary, syntax, and background knowledge.

Let's use this equation to illustrate the point further. If a child's decoding skills are strong, but their *language comprehension* is weak, it will look like this:

$$1 \times 0 = 0$$

In other words, reading comprehension is still 0 despite having strong decoding skills.

Likewise, if a child's decoding skills are weak, but their language comprehension skills are strong, it will look like this:

$$0 \times 1 = 0$$

That is to say the same result despite their language comprehension skills.

If, however, a child's decoding skills are strong and their language skills are also strong, it will look like this:

$$1 \times 1 = 1$$

That is, both decoding and language comprehension are required for reading comprehension. The ability to engage in conversation is the essential prerequisite for a child's developing fluency in spoken language and fluent speech is an essential precursor to reading and writing fluently.

Learning how to listen (receptive language)

If conversations are meant to be an exchange of thoughts and ideas, then the participants need to know how to listen. As most educators can attest, this is easier said than done. It is hard for younger children to listen and attend for long periods of time; they are just not equipped developmentally to do so yet. Improvement comes with practice and with regular conversations. Naturally, the older the children are, the longer they can be expected to sustain attentional focus in a conversation.

Nonetheless, through regular conversations, children are not only getting the continuous practice and opportunity to develop listening skills, but they see the teacher(s) doing the same. The teacher models *active* listening. This is done through eye contact and turning one's shoulders towards the speaker. It is done through gestures such as nodding and follow-up with clarifying questions and statements that show children that their ideas were listened to, intentionally. Modeling this form of listening is more important than one might think, for this is not always the experience that children have when speaking to adults. Through no fault of their own, busy parents try their best to listen, but often are doing so while multi-tasking. This is also true for teachers and other adults that children encounter on a regular basis. Classroom conversations provide a chance for children to see and feel what active listening is and learn how they can do the same.

Naturally, teaching children how to be active listeners cannot be left to modeling alone and needs to be explicitly taught as well. The teacher should thoughtfully establish the behaviors that make conversations possible, such as how to take turns speaking and to show that you are listening. Young children will need to be continuously reminded as they build up these neural networks, these skills and habits of active listening. Listening is an auditory discrimination skill. As such, it is useful to know that it is easier for the brain to get information visually. To me, this means two things 1) auditory discrimination is a skill that needs a lot of practice as it is both difficult and essential to communication and life skills and 2) it is ok to use visual aids to assist in grabbing attention and increasing engagement and understanding.

Increasing vocabulary and other oral language skills

The art of conversation is not the memorization of words and definitions; it is the ability to think, communicate, and understand others. That said, conversations help children build vocabulary, which not only allows for better conversation, but more sophisticated thought. An increased vocabulary also helps to build schemata and content knowledge. There have been numerous studies on the advantage that children from households that support large banks of vocabulary have. But the art of conversation is not simply an exchange of vocabulary words, it is an exchange of sentences with meaning. Through daily conversations, children gain exposure to effective syntax, grammar, and pronunciation. They are also encountering the more nuanced aspects of communication such as cadence, tone, facial, gestural, or vocal animation, intonation, volume, and pitch. And this is a key take away; conversations promote fluency and fluency is evidence of a brain that is listening, processing others' ideas, and formulating their own.

For decades, powerful evidence (Wells, 2009; Hart & Risley, 1995) has demonstrated that children who grow up in families that talk a lot are more likely to do well in school. The evidence of the opposite also holds.

Children who hear fewer words at home can struggle at school. Beyond that crude distinction, studies have also shown that it is not only the quantity of words that foster the child's mind, but also the way words are used. Children who engage in longer conversations more frequently have a leg up in learning how to read. Children seem to prepare for the kind of thinking required to read about the world by having conversations.

In fact, on the level of the brain, young children's exposure to dynamic conversation has been shown to affect the extent to which the *Broca's area* – a part of the brain associated with language production – is active while listening to a story (Romeo, Leonard, et al, 2018). According to Keith Stonvich (1986, 2009), children who know more words will learn more words, and students who read more will learn more from the texts they read. Oral and written language skills are in a positive reciprocating loop, that is elevating one continues to elevate the other. Intentionally incorporating conversations and conversational skills into classroom practice is therefore important for overall literacy skill development, brain development, and identity formation.

Conversations and intellectual curiosity

> It's sobering to realize how many children go through preschool and kindergarten without having the chance to exercise their deductive muscles through meandering conversations with people they like and, instead seem to subsist on a lean diet of passive instruction and inane subjects.
>
> Erika Christakis (2016)

Meandering conversations that promote inquiry on the part of all the participants have the power to directly influence children's intellectual curiosity. Sometimes, it is an intentional open-ended question that prompts a meandering conversation. Engaging in this type of conversational inquiry can teach students that knowledge is worth seeking, and that intellectual pursuits are valuable. Information seeking adds to their emerging constellation of knowledge.

When conversations become comfortable – so that the children do not have to focus too much on the act of speaking and listening – they start to more authentically reflect children's interests and their questions begin to reveal what they are curious about. Teachers can then orchestrate lines of inquiry that lead to project ideas. Conversations become springboards for deep learning and long-term projects. The majority of the long-term projects I have led in my classroom have emerged from organic classroom conversations. For example, one day, a child was sharing a trip he had taken to the mountains with his family with the class. This prompted several children to ask questions about mountains. After collecting their current understanding and the questions they still had, we made a collaborative concept map. This led to a multi-day project in which we researched the ten tallest mountains in the world (taking us all over the globe) and created a mural of the mountains drawn and then painted to scale. We then took a field trip to the closest mountain near our school, Sugarloaf Mountain in Maryland. We hiked to the top and the children took down observations in their sketchbooks about the view and the terrain. Back in the classroom we added Sugarloaf Mountain to our mural and were amazed to see how very tiny it was in comparison to the other mountains even though it had felt like we were up so high! This long-term project would never have happened if I had not allowed this one child to share his random story and then provided the space for children to ask their questions. Likewise, it would never have happened if I hadn't helped the students organize their knowledge and wonderings onto a concept map in which they all contributed.

Dialogic teaching with read alouds

Dialogic simply means 'in dialogue' and so refers to all the moments that we teach in or through dialogues. In the research on language and reading comprehension, *dialogic reading* refers to the use of conversation as a way to increase engagement and comprehension of stories and their components. Through dialogic reading, a teacher can help children understand sequence, plot, the use of grammar and cadence, character identity, the feelings portrayed, vocabulary, etc. Dialogic reading can help children hone skills such as summarizing as well as the more creative and open-ended skills of coming up with their own wonderings and predictions related to the story. This can be done during read-alouds and many teachers do this naturally.

Conversations and the brain

Skills develop as neural networks form and this takes time and repetition, neurons that fire together wire together (see neural plasticity and Hebb's axiom, chapter three). Children must converse repeatedly and regularly in order to build the skills we have been talking about in this chapter. This is best achieved if they feel a sense of belonging while progressing in their ability to articulately and grammatically convey meaning with fluency as well as listening to and processing the ideas shared by others. Over time, children will learn how to connect questions, ideas, wonderings, and knowledge. The skills and dispositions of mind that children gain when they learn how to engage in rich conversations on a regular basis enhance all areas of thinking and content knowledge, as their ability to use and understand vocabulary, speech, social cognition, metacognition, and knowledge of the world increases.

Summary

In sum, classroom conversations are a woefully underutilized pedagogical tool that has the capacity to greatly increase cognitive skills while simultaneously building relationships, belonging, and community. A meaningful conversation is an extended exchange of thoughts and ideas in which the topic holds significance and meaning to the participants. Meaningful classroom conversations hold space for each student to express themself. To that end, such conversations cannot be 'controlled' by the teacher, although they can be flexibly guided. In early childhood, conversations can be meandering as children work towards a shared attentional focus that incorporates the connection of thoughts and ideas in the conversation. As a regular pedagogical and relationship-building tool, conversations help build neural networks, and as this happens the conversations themselves will become more advanced. Here lies another example of a self-reinforcing upward spiral as advanced conversations will in turn further support both oral and written language, organized thinking, collaborative learning, knowledge acquisition, executive functions, belonging, and well-being. Conversations can also increase children's metacognition which has a multiplier effect on all types of learning. Conversations prepare children to think logically as the exchange of ideas motivates children to understand and to be understood, and this should be one of our principle aims in education.

Aligning to Practice

- Early on in the year I introduce the word 'theory', and then use it quite often in sentences like, 'My theory about why _____ is _____. What is your theory?'

- Prompt conversations that invite comparison of two books, objects, or experiences; comparisons require the children to focus on detail as well as organize concepts in their schemata. It also helps them to use information to draw conclusions.

- Help extend and connect learning experiences by retelling the story of learning from the previous day. Ask children to consider what might have changed in their thinking. For example, 'Yesterday, you were really excited about what you and John built on the block rug, but you had to rebuild the foundation so it would not fall over. Can you explain to the rest of the class what you learned and what you might do differently when you build today?' Another example of this could be, 'A lot of excitement was generated when we watched the documentary of how beavers build dams. If you were going to build a dam, what ideas could you borrow from the beavers?'

- Use photos of the children involved in a learning activity to prompt a conversation about what is happening. Oftentimes, children have an easier time reflecting on their learning with the visual aid of a photograph and love to see themselves and their friends in action. A teacher's prompt might be as simple as, 'Describe to me what is happening in this photo.'

- Start with small groups. Five is an ideal number to get conversations and collaborative thinking going. With time we will become more confident in our ability to facilitate rich conversations and provide the best conditions for them as teachers, the children will also likely show greater focus as their own confidence and skills grow.

- Brainstorm questions with colleagues that could stimulate students' curiosity and challenge them to hypothesize or think deeper. This will simultaneously help build the teacher/researcher culture at your school.

Further reading

Christakis, Erika (2016) *The Importance of Being Little: What preschoolers really need from grownups.*

Tomasello, Michael (2019) *Becoming Human: A theory of ontogeny.*

CHAPTER 11:
CO-CREATING A CULTURE OF INTELLECTUAL CURIOSITY AND DEEP THINKING

The greatest thing in our favor was growing up in a family where there was always much encouragement to intellectual curiosity.

Orville Wright (quoted in McCullough, 2016)

Curiosity is an eager desire to know or learn about something. It can be thought of as a desire to fill in a gap in knowledge. In this sense, it is the motivation to make what is unfamiliar, familiar. It can be thought of as extending one's knowledge to make a new connection or as shaking up the ground of one's current knowledge to reveal cracks that need further explanation or understanding. In referring to *intellectual curiosity* and deep thinking for young children, I am referring to the intense and oftentimes, abiding desire to explore and ponder aspects of phenomena for the purpose of making connections and increasing understanding. What, then, is *deep thinking*? Deep thinking is different from regular thinking in that it demands more attention, focus, and leaves more of a residue in our long-term memory. Daniel Willigham states, 'Memory is the residue of thought'. Deep thinking requires more effort and for that reason, leaves us more to hold onto.

Both intellectual curiosity and deep thinking entail a level of cognitive flexibility to rearrange and build upon current knowledge or schemata. How does this new piece of information fit into my current understanding?

This disposition of seeking new information and flexibly accounting for it reflects our adaptability. Recalling concepts from part two of this book in which we talked about human brain development from an anthropological perspective, adaptability has always been important for humans and will continue to be so. 'Educational content will continue to have value, but flexibility will have even more. What graduates know today is becoming less important than what they can learn' (Bowen, 2021). Learning how to learn, staying curious, thinking deeply, and responding adaptively might be a determining factor for success in the future lives of our students. Success in school and work might be the two most concrete reasons why we should value intellectual curiosity and deep thinking, but they are not the only reasons. These attributes are important for a sense of purpose, for well-being, and for a positive disposition of mind towards learning. Curiosity and deep thinking make children's lives more interesting and help create the conditions for them to thrive in a challenging world.

As humans, we practice curiosity everywhere, not just in schools. But it is in schools that we want to engage children with knowledge, the act of seeking knowledge, and the joy associated with attaining it (their disposition of mind). It is, therefore, in schools, from preschool to graduate school, where we need to think of facilitating individual and collective curiosity. This sentiment is powerfully and beautifully stated by Perry Zurn and Dani Bassett (2020):

> [Schools] are spaces in which we gather to commemorate and to create tracks of knowledge. By turns, we lead and follow one another along the furrows, crisscrossing the world of things known and yet to be known. Nevertheless, as academic studies and personal testimonials repeatedly confirm, educational institutions today are consistently threatened with the loss of curiosity, a lagging of wonder, and a dearth of delight in discovery. Too often, compliance and complacency, bureaucratic constraints and mundane deliverables compromise the environments of creative freedom necessary for the pursuit of knowledge. And far too often, social inequalities, ableism, and disciplinary silos build walls between learners, their potentialities, and their communities. It is for these reasons that

learners and educators alike repeatedly ask, By what pathways can the very institutions of curiosity remain curious? How can we imagine learning differently, more equitably? How can these spaces work in concert with the diversity and relational fabric of knowers as the connective tissue of knowledge itself?

Many children begin schooling or formal education with a disposition for learning that is characterized by an enthusiastic curiosity. The cup of their questions overfloweth. Many want to touch things that they are not supposed to touch, take apart things that they are not supposed to take apart, and test cause and effect in ways that stress adults out to no end. We have all witnessed this ebullience in children, and we might even remember when we were this way ourselves. We might be able to think of times in our current lives in which we have felt incredibly motivated and intrigued by what we pursued. Times when the objective and the process of attaining it filled us with a sense of purpose that made the entire endeavor at once challenging, enjoyable, and rewarding. Writing this book has been this way for me.

To the careful observer, the way young children create learning opportunities for themselves is obvious. They gather objects, specimens, observations, and ideas and mull them over. They act out scenarios and practice responses as they take on a variety of roles. They don't have sophisticated spoken language, so they use narrative and metaphor. They find other ways of telling and asking. They use repetition to hone skills and understanding. And according to Susan Engel, they are gathering knowledge and small ideas *for the service of future big ideas*. This is what intellectual curiosity looks like in young children.

Teachers of early childhood education, especially those that teach preschool, will tell you that they often see an active and enthusiastic curiosity in their students. Ask someone who teaches upper elementary school grades the same question, and they will report seeing this type of overt and self-propelled curiosity much less. Continue to middle and high school, and it dwindles still further.

Like all humans, young children are heavily influenced by the experiences and relationships they have. Whether they develop a disposition of mind in which they value the pursuit of deeper understanding is wrapped up in the experiences and feelings that they have had while learning. Remember that emotions drive what we pay attention to and remember, and that emotions also become embedded in the experience itself. Have children been welcomed into a learning community and given voice? Have they been explicitly encouraged by trusted adults to explore and develop their own ideas? Engel states that by the age of six, nearly all children have the skills to concoct their own ideas, but by 8 years old, many no longer demonstrate a motivation to do so. 'An inventory of the work gathered in almost any public school classroom, from kindergarten on, will attest to this. You can find lots of evidence that students are gaining specific skills and acquiring certain facts. But you will see virtually no sign that they are being given time, support, or guidance to pursue their own original ideas or to investigate the existing ideas that captivate them' (Engel, 2021). Gaining skills and acquiring factual knowledge is an important part of schooling and no one would argue with that. However, research supports intentional and explicit encouragement from adults – through the language teachers use, the relationships they build, and the classroom culture that they help to create – as key factors for the development of intellectual curiosity and deep thinking.

The title of this chapter (and of the next two) deliberately uses the term 'co-creating', rather than simply creating. This is to remind the reader that we (adults and children) are all learners, teachers, and creators in collaboration. We all continuously influence each other in profound ways and we all play key roles in the environments, cultures, and dispositions of mind that we co-create and support. Everyone in the school is part of this process of co-creation though their influence will naturally vary in degree.

The drive to explore, curiosity, and dopamine

Dopamine plays a big role in motivation and the reward circuits of the brain (see neurotransmitters and dopamine, chapter three). Researcher Colin DeYoung has referred to dopamine as the 'neuromodulator of exploration' because it is the neurotransmitter that makes us *want* to explore as well as facilitating the cognitive and behavioral processes that support exploration. It would follow then that dopamine plays a role in the moments when our curiosity is sparked and those that follow as we explore what intrigues us. Dopamine facilitates flexible thinking as we engage with novel phenomena (DeYoung, 2013). The role of dopamine in exploration and curiosity is one more indicator of how our brains are hardwired to engage with the world of objects, experiences, and ideas in order to learn.

Theme one: Curiosity and positive identity formation

The relationship between curiosity and student agency

This theme of student agency will come up again in the following chapters on creativity, imagination, and classroom conversations. It plays a crucial role in children's intellectual pursuits as well as their ways of expressing and communicating in the world and is connected to motivation, emotion and cognition, positive identity formation, the emergence of more sophisticated skills, and skill transfer (the ability to bring a skill into another domain). The emergence and coordination of lower level thinking into higher order thinking that then transfers across domains reflect the agency of the child. On the level of the brain, it activates neuronal pathways and strengthens patterns of pathways in our increasingly self-organized brains (Cantor, et al, 2021) and is also connected to other motivational constructs such as interest and persistence. Teachers make pedagogical decisions in the classroom that can either support or discourage agency. Agency-supportive practices would include intentionally creating the space and time to allow for children's voice, interests, and questions. A sense of agency and a trusting relationship with teachers leads to high levels of interest and persistence and 'high levels of interest and persistence predict better academic and social achievement in school' (Spelke & Shutts, 2020). So, whether we are coming at if from a neuroanatomy perspective, a well-being and motivation perspective, or an acquisition of usable and durable knowledge and skills perspective, having agency in learning is crucial.

What are you curious about?

A sense of wonder so indestructible it would last throughout life, as an unfailing antidote against the boredom and disenchantment of later years, the sterile preoccupation with things that are artificial, the alienation from the sources of our strengths.

Rachel Carson (1965)

Young children's curiosity and interests are often unabashedly on display when they walk in the classroom or playground. They show in what catches their attention, what they are wearing, what they are playing, what they are drawing, and the words that come out of their mouths. This is another advantage that early childhood educators have – just observing children provides a treasure trove of information about what their interests are and what makes them tick – and is yet another reason why documenting observations of children is so helpful for getting to know them and planning future lessons. Master teachers take that information and then pose questions to draw out children's curiosity even further. Prompting children with 'I wonder…' questions can get them to tinker with and further develop their own thoughts and ideas. Another strategy is paying close attention to what the child is grappling with and providing words or materials to help that child explore more deeply. This type of scaffolding also allows the teacher to redirect them from misconceptions.

Key to helping children stay curious is exposing them to a plethora of materials, experiences, and experts in a diversity of fields. Guest experts, field trips, and classroom materials should be selected for a diverse range of topics and opportunities. Many mistakenly believe that helping children follow their own interests means leaving them alone to explore and not teaching them skills and knowledge. The opposite is true! Let's give children exposure to how a pastry chef creates new desserts or what hydraulic engineers do. Let's give them the opportunity to interview an architect and discover their process or learn what artists inspired other artists. Let's have them look at different playgrounds around their city or town and then design their own. And let's see what lingering questions they have.

Children who are exposed to many realms of knowledge and experience and are encouraged to follow their interests and lines of inquiry learn that their thoughts, questions, and ideas matter. Supported by teachers and powered by their own curiosity, children solve problems or challenges that they *set for themselves*. Solving problems is rewarding no matter who sets them up, but there is a qualitative difference when a child solves a problem that they care about, that came *from them*. When a child is creating their own problems to solve, they are building upon their interests, their sense of self-efficacy, and their disposition of mind towards learning.

Through curiosity children understand who they are and what they are capable of. This is a powerful idea and one that many educators don't necessarily think of in explicit terms, though they probably do consider as they get to know their students. Helping children develop their own intellectual curiosity is helping children understand who they are. Through their actions and words, teachers can show children that their interests, questions, and strengths (and not just weaknesses) matter. That they can explore and discover meanings at school, and they are inherently capable, knowledgeable, and able to grow that knowledge.

As children get older and go through school, they will likely be exposed to the overwhelming messages from society that grades and scores matter above all else. I feel this amounts to a kind of academic frenzy and it is something I faced raising my own children. I was very intentional about the messages I was giving my own children as they were growing up. I went to great lengths to encourage them to follow their interests, love learning, and see school as a place for opportunity and growth. I told them it is not about the grades. Grades do not accurately relay the whole picture of what a student has learned. I explained that I just wanted them to stay inspired to learn and grow and not take grades too seriously. While in high school, my eldest explained to me that although they remembered the message that I had always given, that was not the message society was telling them. Their experience in middle and upper school in the DC area was being told that grades and scores are *everything*. And my other two teenagers agreed with this sentiment. The message I was giving them was in conflict with the message the world was giving them and that is disheartening.

Focusing on grades and scores seems to begin earlier and earlier in school, especially in some communities, and it is often reinforced by parents, school leaders, and college admissions. It is a great distraction from what school is meant to be. One of my favorite quotes is by Greg

Walton who wrote, 'We should be explicit that school is about learning and growth, not identifying who is smart' (2020). This distraction is pulling children away from knowing themselves, their passions, their sense of meaning and purpose in the world and this is something that should concern all teachers of all grades. It is something that should concern all citizens interested in the future of our country and the world. Stanford psychologist William Damon believes that the biggest problem facing youth today is a sense of meaninglessness. When students don't have the opportunity to connect what they are doing in school to what is meaningful to them, they drift and feel disconnected. Add the academic pressures heaped on children, and the wider challenges the world continues to face, and it is no wonder that they feel the highest levels of stress on record.

Beginning when they are young and first developing their associations with school, we need to foster their interests and intellectual curiosity, so that they know who they are and begin with a disposition of mind that is optimistic for their future growth and learning. And then we need to take care of it, so it does not fade away.

Intellectual curiosity and the development of self-confidence

According to Michele Borba, author of *Thrivers*, self-confidence is the foundational strength that all other important strengths and character traits grow from. Knowing one's own interests and strengths goes hand in hand with having self-confidence. By helping children discover and follow their interests and what they want to learn more about, we are helping them build and acknowledge their own strengths (which may or may not be represented in other parts of the school day). This simultaneously helps them to develop self-confidence which in turn leads to happier children, but also better academic performance and resilience.

Theme two: Deep thinking skills

Deep thinking and intellectual curiosity go together. Without delving too far into ideas and philosophies around deep thinking skills, I want to highlight two relevant categories: independent thinking and collaborative thinking.

Independent thinking

A mind that is encouraged to ask questions and be curious is likely to be one that can think independently. Today's students will be entering a future life and job market in which independent thinking and the ability to adapt and think critically and creatively will matter even more than it does today.

The world is awash with information. While the increased access to information can be good, filtering the reliable from the unreliable on social media, the news, markets, and so on, is a skill in and of itself. Filtering is also complicated. Information is often mediated through social media and therefore it is often presorted for us based on past searches, etc. There is also the issue of confirmation bias, that is our brain's tendency to pay more attention to the information that supports our current convictions and sees information that questions such convictions as threatening. And, lastly, as a social species, humans are culturally and biologically evolved to be heavily swayed by the people around us and what their beliefs are. While this third reason can increase our empathy, awareness, and ability to solve problems, it can also hinder it. Although issues around unreliable news sources and independent thinking are probably not concerns that keep early childhood educators up at night, it is part of our world and the world these children are growing up in.

Collaborative thinking

All children should have ample experience of working towards solutions with a group of peers. We know that we are social beings with social brains and that learning with peers can increase attention for and memory of the material. We also know that children need practice developing their receptive and expressive language skills, and there is no better place to practice these skills than in collaboration on a shared goal. So, how do we elicit intellectual curiosity and deep thinking in collaboration? There are intentional and well thought out ways of setting up collaborative learning experiences and less intentional, less successful ways. While teachers will want to make sure the children are doing the 'heavy lifting,' teachers should be close enough to the collaborations to be able to jump in, support, scaffold, and make sure all members have ways to contribute. For an inspirational example of how this can be done in the adult world, let's turn to the MIT Media Lab.

The MIT Media Lab bases their practice of innovation on four principles: peers, passion, projects, and play. These Labs will involve computer scientists, musicians, neurobiologists, designers, artists, biomedical engineers, and architects all working together to find innovative solutions to human problems. The intellectual diversity of the members is deliberate as multiple perspectives and areas of knowledge are sought to elevate not only the product (goal), but the thinking of all members. In this atmosphere, curiosity flourishes as members build upon each other's ideas. Projects fall apart, things don't go as planned, and once promising ideas get scrapped, but this is to be expected as part of the process. Absorbed by their curiosity and their shared goal, these innovation brainstorms have led to creations like Siri, e-readers, the programming language Scratch, and Lego Mindstorm robots to name some. If the scholars, experts, and researchers at MIT Media Labs see the value of this type of collaborative problem solving, why wouldn't educators see and take advantage of the same ideas (i.e. peers, passion, projects, and play)?

Theme three: Sowing the seeds

How do we intentionally create classroom cultures that sow the seeds of intellectual curiosity and deep thinking? Teachers of younger children in the beginning of preschool can attest to their students' ability to hop from the role of adventurous explorer to inspired scientist, imaginative innovator, armchair philosopher, expressive artist, and back again. This kind of embodied curiosity and deep thinking is experienced through whole-hearted role play and is part of childhood. Toddlers engage in this kind of active inquiry and investigation before they are even able to articulate what it is they are exploring or even what role they are playing. Oftentimes, the idea itself is not fully developed, but is just a seed. Early childhood is and ought to be a time for sowing seeds for many ideas.

Seeds are sown in different ways. Children engage in active observation, collect and manipulate objects as a way of seeking information, or in the pursuit of a question or wondering. We are not always able to ascertain the motivator behind a child's interest, but the seeking behavior itself 'hints at an important feature of young children's emerging intellectual lives' (Engel, 2021): their drive to be agents in answering their own plentiful questions. Just like babies and toddlers, young children are constantly investigating to make the unfamiliar familiar, but by the middle of their third year, most children have a powerful new tool to aid them. They can now put words together to ask questions. Depending on the child and their own developmental timeline, language becomes more and more central to their investigations and engagement with understanding the world around them.

The psychologist Michelle Chouinard (2007) followed four young children and the questions they asked from the age of three to the age of five. Through regular recordings, she amassed 24,741 questions over 229.5 hours. As one can imagine, the children asked questions for different reasons, including to get attention, to seek permission, and to request some action from an adult. However, more than seventy percent of their questions reflected a desire for information. Their questions also changed as they became older, and by the age of five they asked more questions that required explanations for events, objects, and conversations. Questions increasingly included why and how. Preschool and kindergarten become important years for children to use language in the pursuit of more knowledge.

With this foundational knowledge and our intentions, we can recognize and value how our young students are expressing their curiosity. We can now see and understand how they are thinking deeply, and we can begin to foster it even more. Now we can use Mind, Brain, and Education concepts, and our professional experience supported by our relationships with the children, to elevate both their and our own curiosity. Our classroom can become a space full of researchers.

In 2022, in a conversation with Jennifer Azzariti, atelierista (in the Reggio Emilia approach this is a studio teacher with formal education in the arts) and pedagogical director, I asked how Reggio Emilia-inspired schools are able to create a lively culture of wonder and research. She said:

> The desire to research can be generated through engagement in creative processes which more often than not bring us into situations of uncertainty and even confusion. In a rich and

complex learning environment, questions emerge and we want to know more. Why? What if? How might …? Hand in hand with having questions is also cultivating an environment where it is safe to ask questions, when wondering is encouraged and even expected.

In this kind of classroom, a spirit of inquiry and research is part of the children and teachers' way of learning together. Jennifer went on to explain how the process of documenting children's words, behaviors, and artworks generates material for teachers to analyze 'which always leads to more questions, revealing further paths of inquiry and exploration'.

At the beginning of this book, I explained that working at Reggio Emilia-inspired schools was part of my early career in education. I have gone on to work at other excellent schools with varying mission statements, philosophies, and cultures. However, the residue from my early exposure to Reggio Emilia principles and guiding beliefs, especially regarding intellectual curiosity, continue to inspire the work that I do.

Asking questions

Many teachers have told me that elementary aged children quickly gain skills in summarizing content but have a harder time asking their own original questions regarding that very content. At first glance, this is surprising because it seems like less of a cognitive lift to come up with a question than to attend, store information in working memory, comprehend, make connections, and construct a summary. But coming up with an original question is a *creative* process and as such benefits from practice and explicit encouragement. We need to ask children 'what questions do you have?' instead of 'does anyone have a question?' We need to make space for questions, validate them, be explicit about their value to learning, and be comfortable admitting when we don't know the answers. Showing a child that their question has inspired a teacher to investigate further is a powerful thing.

In his book, *A More Beautiful Question*, long-time journalist, Warren Berger explores the power of inquiry to propel growth in business as well as in our personal lives. Through his own extensive research including interviews with some of the world's leading innovators and creative minds, Berger makes a compelling argument that their successes lie in their ability to question. He suggests that the breakthrough inventions and radical solutions his interviewees have made can often be attributed to their ability to pose different questions. In speaking to educators, Berger found that many of them agree that the skill of asking questions is critically important and will likely be 'even more important in the future as complexity increases and change accelerates' (2014). Most educators, however, describe their school culture as one that explicitly values answers over questions. In 2023, educators had to start grappling with AI engines like ChatGPT and this phenomenon, is showing us in real time the value of knowing how to ask the right questions.

Questioning as a habit and skill tapers off as children get older and that is not all due to school's influence. Remember, the brain is a metabolically expensive tissue, and it naturally looks for ways to reduce workload. This is why the brain identifies and registers patterns. It might also be why, after a period of time, the process of continually questioning and seeking new understanding becomes superfluous and counter to the brain's desire to make sense in an efficient manner. Allowing your brain to go into 'auto pilot', might allow students and workers alike to focus on the task at hand, or in many cases, the several tasks at hand. However, the constant change we face as humans living today will likely not slow down when our children are adults. The likelihood is that change will be continuous, challenging, and complex, which means we might be forced to spend less time in autopilot. As Berger suggests, we might be forced to spend 'more time in questioning mode – attempting to adapt, looking to re-create careers, redefining old ideas about living, working, and retiring, reexamining priorities, seeking new ways to be creative, or to solve various problems in our own lives or the lives of others' (Berger, 2014).

If asking questions helps us make sense of the world, identify problems, and create new opportunities, then why don't we teach or encourage more questioning? Why, in fact, do children dramatically decrease the number of questions they ask when they begin schooling? Is there something we can be doing differently? These questions lead me to ask, are we unintentionally shackling children's questions and in so doing, not giving them practice formulating good questions? Asking questions that lead to new and deeper understanding is a skill, and one that we would hope children get to practice at school.

Being able to come up with one's own questions is important in a multitude of ways. So far, we have talked about it as a necessary skill for learning, creative thinking, innovation, and success in school and work. But paying attention to questions does something else as well. Children's questions give us – teachers and parents – windows into their intellectual lives and if we are interested in cultivating their intellectual curiosity, we should be looking for these windows. Gliding over their questions shuts out the wealth of information contained within them, their interests, yes, but also how they are conceptualizing and building knowledge. By encouraging and paying attention to children's questions we can better understand how to support their understanding and growth and this, in turn, informs how we support, scaffold, and plan next steps/lessons/learning experiences. It can also nurture the type of disposition of mind which we aim to cultivate.

Questions like rivers and tributaries

Is there a connection between children's *why* and *how* questions and their later cognitive endeavors? Meredith Rowe and her colleagues analyzed conversations between US fathers and their young children. They looked at the questions that fathers asked of their toddlers and then revisited those same children a few years later. 'The children whose fathers had asked more *why* and *how* questions when they had just learned to talk know more and showed higher-level cognitive functions when they were in preschool' (Engel, 2021). The implication of Rowe's data appears to suggest that the exchanges between parent and child can have immediate and long-term effects on the child's thinking. Although this study did not involve teachers, we can extrapolate that the same *probably* holds true for teachers and children as well. It is quite possible that the type of questions that children are encouraged to ask and ponder 'has a formative influence on the habits of thinking that children acquire' (Engel, 2021).

Curiosity and connections to prior knowledge

Whether the topic is new and intriguing to the children or a continuation of one explored in the past, children will learn more if they are able to make connections to what they already know. The brain relies on neural pathways that were previously forged. From these neural pathways, children can create denser neural connections while building deeper and more nuanced knowledge. Children's prior knowledge helps them to anchor new understandings, new ideas, and new concepts.

Delightfully serious: Philosophy with young children

Just as children have a natural proclivity towards approaching life as a scientist, so too are they natural philosophers. They don't just love small questions and probing. They love big questions well. Yes, philosophy can be serious, but it is also about being playful with ideas and assumptions. It is being creative about words and concepts. It is about turning things upside down and inside out in order to examine them and deepen our understanding. Young children should engage in philosophical discussions! In leading (not teaching) philosophical discussions with elementary aged children, Jana Mohr Lone notes, 'children's questioning can constitute the most primary of philosophical activities: reflecting on the meaning of ordinary experiences and concepts in order to develop an understanding of the world, others, and themselves' (Lone, 2021). Children's philosophical questions reveal important aspects of their concerns and current understanding, but also their yearning for deeper and broader understanding. Through her work, Lone engages children in philosophical thinking using prompts such as the meaning of happiness, justice and fairness, individuality and community, and the nature of beauty. I remember when I was young being so perplexed about the continuous motion of time: that in just writing this sentence, my present is already my past. I distinctly remember a recurring question I asked myself, 'If I were to write the word 'time' large enough that it would take infinity to write it, what would it look like?' This question would drive anyone mad because it is impossible to answer and yet I remember that the question itself gave me a feeling of awe. It still does. Philosophical wondering begins in childhood.

Years ago, the four and five-year-olds I was teaching and I had several philosophical conversations about happiness. I asked them: what is happiness? what does it feel like? and how can we attain it? Their ideas became pages in a book that we created for the parents and school community. One child stated, 'To be happy, everyone needs to play in nature and take care of it. Trees make oxygen and animals keep the earth alive and happy.' The way he connected those concepts as a five-year-old are probably different than how he would connect them now as a sixteen-year-old. Would he still say that animals keep the earth alive and happy? Nonetheless, in his confident statement, he connected concepts of human happiness to the earth's happiness. He also connected happiness to play, nature, oxygen, health, and having a role or sense of purpose in taking care of things outside of himself. This is quite profound! While this exercise was insightful for the adults, it also provided an opportunity for the children to think hard about a topic everyone refers to, but often take for granted. It was questioning with inherent purpose and allowed for them to make an emotional connection to a concept while practicing how to construct philosophical statements and wonderings with words. And they were learning from and about each other in a way that young children often do not get the chance. Lone states, 'Being a child shouldn't mean being treated as a mediocre thinker'. Children's capacity for deep thinking around the most basic elements of life is greater than many think. Through this level of inquiry, we can get them to think hard in reflective and meaningful ways, ways that promote further inquiry and deep thinking. Let them associate school as a place where we can ponder and discuss big ideas.

Emergent curricula

When students feel a sense of control over their own learning process, a much wider range of learning can occur – this is because when children are intrinsically motivated about a topic, problem-solving, creativity, analysis, synthesis, critical thinking, and decision making are more likely to occur. These are all higher-level cognitive skills that involve developing neural networks in their prefrontal cortex. Naturally, topics that children care about are inherently meaningful and therefore, purposeful to them. According to Michelle Borba, 'Purpose-driven activities have a multiplier effect because they can increase kids' self-confidence, empathy, integrity, self-control, curiosity, perseverance, and optimism' (2021). 'Emergent curricula' is the practice of creating learning opportunities based on the interests of the specific children in one's class. An obvious benefit to this practice is that it is inherently purpose-

driven, motivating, and engaging. Another benefit is the ε
the questions that arise from the children as they get dee
emergent curriculum project. There are, however, several challenges ...
require teachers to think hard, be open-minded, and strategic.

The first challenge is the potential quantity of diverging interests.
Attending to the curiosities and interests of *all* the students lands
somewhere between tricky and impossible. At least, it seems that way.
But I have been using emergent curricula for over 20 years in classrooms
and have learned about the trials and tribulations as well as strategies
and successes from my mentors and colleagues. I have found a general
process that helps set you up for success. Observing children during
play and in conversation (whether whole class, small group, or one-
on-one) is a starting point. This is where you are most likely to pick up
on their passions, curiosities, and developing ideas. Meanwhile, set up
provocations in the classrooms. Design interesting learning experiences
and field trips and watch what children do with them. Next, engage in
discussion with colleagues to explore perceived interests and potential
project ideas that will help the class delve deeper. Don't be afraid to
question the educational worth and value of different proposed ideas
as the purpose of this brainstorm is to land on a well-developed and
inspired idea. Next, test it out. Begin the project. Does it garner the
interest of some, but not all the children? If that is the case, consider
making it a project for those interested and explore a different idea for
the other group. This is where I like to set up committees of children
with like interests and project goals. Excitement among young children
can be very contagious so peers can be the motivating factors to get
more children actively engaged in a project. Remember, though, some
ideas just fail. That is ok too. It is ok to back away from a project that you
thought would get everyone engaged when you see that it is not working.
Return to dialogue with your colleagues and come up with something
new.

The second challenge is equity. While some children make their
obsession with dinosaurs boldly known and acknowledged by all, other
children's interests are lesser known. And that is why continuing to
develop strong relationships of trust with those children, presenting
possibilities in the form of books and provocations in the classroom,

as well as dialogue with parents, and fellow teachers will help. Whether their interests announce themselves or are more subtly expressed, it is these interests that will guide their efforts and curiosity and that teachers can use to nurture the pursuit of knowledge for its own sake.

The third and fourth challenges are time and flexibility. It takes time to follow the steps needed to make an emergent curricula topic successful. Incorporating different modalities to help build robust neural networks as part of the project only adds to the time spent on planning and execution. There needs to be a shared belief among the teachers that it is worth this extra time, and the acceptance that they might have to get creative in how they go about finding it. Sometimes, that means finding overlap and cross-disciplinary ways to merge learning goals, something that becomes more of a challenge in kindergarten than preschool. And this is obviously connected to the need for flexibility as the projects unfold, observations are made, and ways of deepening the learning become more apparent. However, the relative unpredictability of emergent curricula is part of what makes it engaging for teachers. We are all becoming more curious together; about the topic, how far we can take it, and what new and exciting connections and experiences it could lead to.

Many are skeptical of this approach, asking what happens to the skills and information the children need to have if teachers and students are spending all of their time just following their interests? This is a good question. Preplanned curricula are based on the belief that teachers already know what children need to learn, what they will be able to learn, and how they will best learn it before they have even gotten to know the children. But just as every child is different, every class is different, and every day presents different opportunities and challenges. It is, in many ways, easier to just follow a curriculum guidebook. With emergent curricula, however, one is only bound by our own limits of creative thinking to find ways of teaching the skills and information that children need to know in a given year. Teacher/researchers pay attention to MBE strategies and concepts, general curricular goals, as well as the interests and needs of the children and then design curricula, lessons, and experiences in responsive and creative ways.

Theme four: The teacher/researcher that models and supports

Students are heavily influenced by the dispositions of mind, thinking habits, styles, and personalities of their teachers. Oftentimes, the teachers that students say they remember are those that made the teacher-student relationship a priority and those that had passion for their subject. As early childhood educators, we know the power of our relationships with our students and modeling. Children learn from our actions and attitudes not just from our words. A teacher who exudes a healthy intellectual curiosity is bound to influence the development of a student's disposition towards learning and their own intellectual curiosity. How do you do that? Be intellectually curious yourself. Bring your interests and passions into the classroom in developmentally appropriate ways. Share stories of your learning, both present and past. Admit a lack of knowledge and understanding if a child asks a question to which you do not know the answer. Invite the children to assist you in your research to address that question. In doing so, you are also validating the student's question, which has its own benefits. Verbalize explicitly what new knowledge you have gained. Explain how a strategy or lesson idea might address a question you have about learning yourself. Solicit ideas from the students about their goals and experiences. Model and explicitly discuss the use and value of observation, documentation, collaboration, and iteration in both student and teacher learning.

Teaching young children is different from teaching any other age group in significant ways. When it comes to how best to support inquiry, intellectual curiosity, and deep thinking, it is important to consider a few of those differences. When young children come to us in preschool and kindergarten, they come with the spirit and drive for active exploring, questioning, and research. However, language acquisition, both expressive and receptive, is still developing and there will be a wide range of language skills and abilities in the classroom. They will also have, in general, lower thresholds for sustained focus and attention than older children. Therefore, how we incorporate direct instruction is not going to be the same for this age group – and will also vary significantly between three and six-year-olds. Understanding the appropriate amount of direct instruction for early childhood is important when trying to foster their own inquiry, intellectual curiosity, and research. Explanations provided by teachers, guest experts, museum guides, and non-fiction books are beneficial and can be wonderful catalysts for further investigations. However, those didactic experiences need to be balanced by ample hands-on opportunities that allow for children to do their own exploring and pondering. We want children to get comfortable with considering facts and formulating their own theories rather than simply giving them all the answers. 'The role of the early years educator is not to transmit current scientific, or historical, or geographical knowledge, but to help young children on their first step to becoming scientists, historians, or geographers. This inquiry learning approach engages the children and makes their learning in these areas meaningful and much more likely to be remembered' (Whitebread & Sitabkhan, 2020). This approach is largely a matter of the language we use to support their investigations as well as how we create balance.

These ideas are illustrated in a study by Engel and Randall (2009) in which teachers were invited into the lab and provided with materials and a worksheet to conduct a science activity called Bouncing Raisins. The activity involved mixing several ingredients into a beaker, dropping a raisin in, and watching while bubbles form on the surface of the raisin, causing it to rise to the surface. Unbeknown to the teachers, the children were also given Skittles and encouraged to drop one in as well at some point during the experiment. In one condition, when the researchers explained the activity to the teachers, they said, 'Please use the materials to help your student learn more about science', and as they left the room, they said, 'have fun learning about science'. In a second condition, the researchers said to teachers, 'Please use the materials to help your student fill out the worksheet', and as they left, the room they said, 'Have fun filling out the worksheet'. The results showed that no matter their age, their level of teaching experience, or their gender, when teachers were encouraged to focus on learning about science, they responded encouragingly to the children's curiosity about what would happen if a Skittle were also dropped in. If they focused on the worksheet, teachers explicitly discouraged other experimentation. In further iterations of the experiment, teachers were encouraged to be experimental and curious themselves while interacting with the children and the materials. The results showed that teachers had an enormous impact on the children's level of engagement and curiosity if they both used language to encourage inquiry *and* modeled it themselves.

Hearing a teacher or parent try out an idea and narrate their thinking is similar to tinkering with a broken machine, and children will learn the value of both by seeing the adults in their lives engaging in this way. A child that is encouraged to give time and attention to their own ideas will likely grow to be an adult that gives time and attention to their own ideas. If we are concerning ourselves with the intellectual lives of children, we must actively and explicitly communicate that encouragement.

Keeping intellectual curiosity alive

In his book, *The Power of Play*, David Elkind describes a condition that he calls 'intellectually burned syndrome'. When he was actively engaged in clinical practice, parents would bring their children to him stating that they were 'bored' or 'unmotivated'. In their sessions, these children told him about their classroom experiences and the collection of these different accounts presented a pattern to Elkind. They described times in which they were intensely involved in a project of interest that was then interrupted or stopped by a teacher or parent. After several experiences of this kind the child simply learned it was best to avoid getting involved in a self-initiated project that they found interesting. They learned to avoid being 'intellectually involved'. Unwittingly, and certainly unintentionally, schools were communicating a message about the value of these children's interests. This could then affect how these children viewed their own interests, as they learned that these were of little worth to others. This could also affect their sense of self-efficacy and the level of trust between them and their teacher. We have all been here! On both ends, probably. We have likely all had the experience at some point in our lives of having a passion or interest interrupted due to someone else's value judgment of its worth. I have also been on the other side more times than I can count, when I have needed children to move onto another lesson. The question then becomes, how do we interrupt these moments, when necessary, without squelching children's intellectual curiosity, drive, and ability to focus and concentrate for long stretches of time? In my experience, it takes a combination of things: more flexibility in the moment, an organization of time that allows for self-initiated projects within the schedule, a consistent system of messaging that stresses the importance of children's interests and passions, a system that allows for projects to be set on pause (but returned to at a later time), and, of course, validating the child's feelings about the interruption while reiterating the logic behind why there is a need to move on in the moment. It is important to keep in mind that children will necessarily have to engage in lessons that they do not find inherently interesting no matter how well we teach them. Being a student does come with a sense of duty, and that does in itself help children learn necessary skills to aid in all sorts of further learning. However, we do not want their days to be full of 'dutiful learning', for that will not foster the disposition of mind that we ultimately want for them in how they view their relationship with school, with teachers, and with learning as a whole.

Dacher Keltner has been looking at awe and how it influences both physical and emotional well-being as well as cognition and dispositional ways of approaching learning. The feeling of awe is hard to describe and Keltner refers to several varieties in his books. Awe is closely linked to admiration and arises when we witness something that helps us see ourselves as a small part of a larger whole. His studies show that experiences of awe enhance wonder, questioning, and curiosity. An experience of awe can arise by simply noticing the intricate veins of a leaf, the height of an old tree, or the generosity of a friend or teacher. Keltner avers that people who feel even only five minutes of awe a day 'are more curious about art, music, poetry, new scientific discoveries, and philosophy' (2023). Furthermore, Keltner's laboratory studies have captured how awe can lead to more rigorous thought, being more discerning between strong and weak arguments, and open to other perspectives. I am struck by the overlap of Keltner's findings and those of other cognitive scientists and educators (including my own) in connecting feelings of awe and wonder to a more abiding disposition towards learning and a desire for deep thinking. So, what can we do to help keep intellectual curiosity alive in our classrooms? Keltner's work suggests that one thing we can do is intentionally design small moments of awe or wonder into our classes to inspire young minds to seek to understand the systems of life and their part in them. We don't need to take them to Mount Everest for this, we can think of ways to bring these moments in our classrooms or in the natural environment surrounding our school building.

Intellectual curiosity and making mistakes

It has been several years now since Carol Dweck published *Mindset* and since then there has been a consistent effort among educators to talk about the value of making mistakes. Mistakes are a necessary part of learning so if we care about learning then we need to communicate to *and convince* children that mistakes are part of the journey. We have slogans and posters on walls about how mistakes are ok. We point to successful inventors and innovators and elaborate on their mistakes to prove our point. And yet, the message is not being received because we are not being completely authentic. It is becoming another thing that 'adults say, but don't really mean'. Starting in kindergarten and sometimes earlier, children are exposed to a curriculum that is divided into subjects. Most subjects teach that there is one correct answer. Children pick up pretty quickly that it is their job to give the correct answer and that other answers are incorrect and therefore, to be avoided. And adults respond differently to correct and incorrect answers. It is not difficult to understand why children might hear adults saying mistakes are ok but still understand that their task is to discover the one correct answer. The other message that goes along with this is the idea of what being smart is. Being smart is often understood as being right, and being right is knowing that single correct answer. Here lies a conundrum.

The reality is that there are correct and incorrect answers to many, though not all, questions. But years of schooling that advertently, or inadvertently, communicate and reinforce this idea of smart equals finding the one correct answer does little to promote the intellectual values that we celebrate. It does not help to encourage multiple perspectives, risk taking, speculation, and active interpretation. This is another area in which the arts can contribute to a healthy disposition towards growth and understanding. Visual image, dance, and music are non-literal forms of representation and can reinforce those same values that other subjects and forms of representation can discourage.

Creating the equitably curious classroom

Authors, Zurn and Bassett have been focusing on the topic of curiosity and more specifically how to create the conditions that promote 'the dynamic force of curiosity equitably' in schools. In their book, *Curious*

Minds, they take the reader on a philosophical and almost poetic path in describing 'The wandering tracks, the weaving concepts, the knitting of ideas, and the thatching of knowledge systems', that characterize curiosity. However, alongside this they also offer a scientific lens, describing the brain structures involved in different types of curiosity. They make the case for equitable access to the rewarding feelings, knowledge, and experiences that accompany the act of following one's own curiosity. As we discussed in chapter five, learning is inherently messy and complex. While we might want to simplify the process for the average student, this leads to problems associated with ignoring sociocultural differences, learning differences, and neurodiversity, while also inhibiting belonging and motivation which, in turn, promotes stereotypes and division. Curiosity thrives in all manners of diversity. It can bring together and connect groups of students (and people, in general). Instead of asking who is curious, teachers should be asking what is each student curious about? Is there a way to better democratize curiosity in the classroom?

What happens when teachers consider it part of their job to cultivate a sense of wonder in the children they work with? Or when children are invited to notice, look closely, play with, and inquire about everyday phenomena that often go unnoticed? How about when children are encouraged to slow down, reflect, and share their thinking? Fleeting interactions become sustained and then become intentional investigations, supported by a learning community and the care and scaffolding of a skilled teacher/researcher.

In this kind of classroom experiences and ideas build upon each other. Through conversations, explorations, and encounters that acknowledge each child – who they are and what they are interested in – teachers can create pathways of knowledge and idea building. The inquisitive disposition that comes naturally to most children can be further developed to create the disposition of mind for current and future learning and development. Supporting intellectual curiosity and deep thinking for all children begins with a knowledge of what curiosity is, why it is important, and continues with the intention of the teacher to keep it growing.

Theme five: The relationship between curiosity and creativity

I am setting myself up here with a title so grandiose one could write volumes on the subject, but I do want to touch upon this relationship and present this idea in a nuanced way as it pertains to early childhood education.

Young children are rapidly building up conceptual understanding alongside their vocabulary. Many young children are also learning how to use the muscles in their mouths and throats to articulate sounds and developing phonological awareness to hear and distinguish different sounds. But even before all of those expressive and receptive language skills are in place, they have wonderous ideas, feelings, and questions. They also have theories and the ability to build upon an idea with another more advanced one. For this reason, young children should be encouraged to not only express but inquire and theorize with their hands. What do I mean by that? For example, consider a child who has noticed that all of the trees in a given area lose their leaves over the same week. This child questions this fact and is curious. You might then invite the child to show their idea or theory as to why that is true through drawing, paints, or clay. Working with the medium gives the child an opportunity to develop their ideas and theories, while in the creative process. The child now has a prompt to help explain (thereby furthering their oral language development) to the class or the teacher what their idea or theory is.

As I laid out at the beginning of this book, curiosity leads to creativity for oftentimes curious minds also have a drive to imagine and conjure up mental imagery of that we have not yet seen, make unique connections, and use different forms of representation to express a feeling or another way of conceiving. This is how we, as humans, broaden and deepen knowledge, create, innovate, imagine better outcomes, collaborate, and seek peace and understanding.

Summary

The best thing we can do to help children love learning is to take their interests seriously. This chapter is about intellectual curiosity and deep thinking. It is about asking big questions. And one of my continuous and guiding big questions as an educator is: how do we foster an engagement with the world that encourages curiosity and deep thinking, creativity and imagination, a sense of purpose, and an inspiration to connect with others? It is a question that has followed me through childhood and is at the core of my years as an educator, a parent, and as a human. Supporting children's intellectual curiosity and deep thinking is made possible through the relationships we form and the experiences we take time to create. It is possible through practices such as emergent curricula, the language we use to support and extend their questions and interests, and by providing the flexibility to allow children space and time to engage in inquiry and theory-building. Cultivating intellectual curiosity and deep thinking is not only possible, but MBE research shows that it is linked to agency, motivation, positive identity formation, knowledge building, achievement, self-confidence, life skills, and a healthy disposition of mind towards learning.

Perry Zurn agreed to meet with me to talk about curiosity, early childhood, education, and this book. After a bit of confusion and a parking snafu, I found my way to his office door. Unbeknownst to me (for I had not checked my most recent email), he was meeting me elsewhere, but there I was in front of his door where this quote was carefully tacked to the door:

> Curiosity as restless questioning, as movement toward the revelation of something hidden, as a question verbalized or not, as search for clarity, as a moment of attention, suggestion, and vigilance, constitutes an integral part of the phenomenon of being alive. There could be no creativity without the curiosity that moves us and sets us patiently impatient before a world that we did not make, to add to it something of our own making.
>
> Paulo Freire (1998)

I had read *Pedagogy of Freedom* early in my education to become a teacher so I must have read this exact excerpt before. But, at this point this quote was a 'drop the mic' moment for me. It captures exactly why curiosity and creativity are connected and why they are so essential to education and 'being alive.'

Alignment to Practice

- Show interest in what children are attending to and make suggestions that will extend their ideas and explorations.

- Make 'I wonder. . .' statements to encourage curiosity, theorizing, and engaged problem solving.

- Explicitly encourage questions with statements like: 'I love your question', 'Your question is helping all of us think about this more', or 'That is a great question, let's find out'.

- Use your hand as a tool to solve problems! This idea was adopted from Michele Borba (2021) and is ingenious. Regardless of the problem (social conflict, disappointment, or academic-in-nature), teach your students to hold up their thumb and 'say the problem'. Next, hold up the pointer, middle, and then ring finger and 'name a possible solution on each finger'. When you get to the pinky, 'Choose the best idea and do it'. If that idea didn't work well, choose one of the others. Not only does this help prompt and then organize their thinking, but it puts them in a position of power as they can come up with solutions themselves. It also encourages iterative thinking if one solution does not work (as happens in life!).

- Go on nature walks with an intention that fosters both focus and open-ended discovery. For example, ask your children to focus on color and tones in nature and have them either take photos, draw pictures, or collect specimens as they walk. Another version is to invite the children to focus on texture. Back in the classroom, have children talk about their discoveries in small and/or whole class groups. Is there a way to document their observations and discoveries to keep their intellectual curiosity going?

- Look at your environment through the lens of these three questions:
  - Does the classroom promote interaction?
  - Does the classroom invite sustained shared thinking?
  - Does the classroom invite collaboration?

  If the answers to any of these is 'no', what can you change?

Further reading

Engel, Susan (2021) *The Intellectual Lives of Children.*

Hopkins, Rob (2019) *From What is To What if: Unleashing the power of imagination to create the future we want.*

Zurn, Perry and Dani S. Bassett (2022) *Curious Minds: The power of connection.*

CHAPTER 12:
CO-CREATING A CULTURE OF CREATIVITY AND IMAGINATION

The impulse to create seems to come naturally to the human brain. However, we must be encouraged to express it. In schools, it's hard to be creative when convergent thinking – the ability to remember facts and perform well on standardized tests – is most highly rewarded. To engage children and prepare them for the workforce, they must be given more opportunities and encouragement to be creative.

Marc Brackett (2019)

Education, in turn, is the process of learning to create ourselves, and it is what the arts, both as a process and as the fruits of that process, promote. Work in the arts is not only a way of creating performances and products; it is a way of creating our lives by expanding our consciousness, shaping our dispositions, satisfying our quest of meaning, establishing contact with others, and changing a culture.

Elliott Eisner (2002)

Curiosity often leads to creativity and vice versa. Curiosity invites inquiry and experimentation. Creativity is the process of putting those ideas and questions together to make unique connections. Curiosity and creativity together reveal new options, new possibilities for thinking, making, and communicating. Our society touts the importance of creativity and innovation. In fact, it is often something we feel a sense of pride in. Many would go as far as to say it is one of our cultural values. Yet, when we look at most schools and most school systems, there is a stark and discouraging disparity. Despite the emphasis we place on the importance of creativity and innovation, very little is being done to create the conditions for children to develop these skills. *We lack creativity about how to support creativity.* I think there are many reasons for this and of course there is wide variability across schools and counties. However, in this chapter, I focus on why these skills are crucial for learning as well as for finding meaning, purpose, and success in school and life.

Encouraging children to be able to represent and communicate their ideas and thoughts through the full range of symbolic systems (words, music, movement, clay, paint, etc.) is one of the key elements in early childhood education. Using the Torrance Test for Creative Thinking (TTCT), Kyung Hee Kim has gathered information about kindergarten through senior year students' ability to respond to situations in novel and original ways. Her studies suggest that creativity in schools may be in trouble. Creative thinking and IQ rose concomitantly until 1990. However, since a point between 1990 and 1998, IQ continued to rise, while creativity has been in a persistent decline. Her analyses broke down different skills related to creativity such as the ability to: generate a large number of unique ideas, deal with hidden aspects of problems, work out the meaningful details of ideas, connect seemingly irrelevant ideas, be open-minded about opposing views, and more. She writes, 'To me, the most troubling aspect of this decreasing creativity is its prevalence in young children who should be actually improving their creative attitudes and skills' (Kim, 2016). Granted, much time has passed since this study and the subsequent article was published, but Kim was interviewed more recently and discussed the fact that as of her more recent analysis of the data in 2018, creativity in the United States is still on the decline. That should be sounding some serious alarm bells. While Kim has theorized causes and discusses connections to this decline in her work, she wants to focus on change, not blame. 'I want to be positive. I still think we can change this' (quoted in Hopkins, 2018). I do too.

So, what does it mean to be creative?

All children have the capacity to be creative. Creativity is not just a skill set. It is also a way of engaging in the world, and of seeing, producing, and generating ideas. Through the creative process, children see the world as full of possibilities and themselves as productive agents in that world. Creativity requires tinkering. That might be with a material, or in a more abstract sense, as with a set of ideas or concepts. It might be the storyline of imaginative play. It might be more tangible as with the products of visual arts, engineering, writing, etc. It might be focused on their other senses as with in music, movement, and other performing arts. Part of an active and healthy creative repertoire includes skills such as risk-taking and originality, reflective practice, inner and outer exploration, and making connections. While creativity is not bound to any one discipline, certain disciplines do help to cultivate it.

Another important aspect of being creative is that it honors individual agency, independent thinking, and making unique connections, but also community and connections between people. Creative expression is often a way of solving a problem or communicating an idea, feeling, or concept to other people. For older children and adults, our creativity might include working with others whether that be in our immediate world of direct experience or engaging with the work of creators from the distant past.

Finding ways to be creative and expressing oneself artistically is the opposite of indifference. In the creative act, children are sometimes just exploring a media, other times, they have a specific idea, story, or feeling to communicate, or their goal or idea might transform as they work. In all of these examples, however, they are engaged and there is a focus and attention on growing, extending, and communicating.

What about imagination?

Creativity, imagination, and innovation are linked. Imagination is the exercise of 'what if?' The act of imagining allows one to create a mental simulation of what could be. As such, acts of imagination naturally support children's insights, discoveries, and creativity. They allow children to rehearse and manipulate ideas thereby impacting memory, attention, and executive function skills. Children practice imagination through artmaking as well as in other forms of play, with the most obvious one being dramatic play.

Imagination is not just for children. We all imagine realities before we work to manifest them. I imagined this book, what I wanted to communicate, who would read it, and how it might make a positive difference in a teacher or child's life. I often imagine how a new project or field trip might excite, inspire, ignite, or deepen learning for children before I plan it out. You do the same. My colleagues imagined a center (the Center for Transformative Teaching and Learning) that would present research from Mind, Brain, and Education to help teachers and students elevate their teaching and learning, and then they planned it out, founded it, and reached international audiences. I am obviously picking examples from my immediate experience, but one could think of any extraordinary and impactful project and think of how it started as an imagined idea. Need I make a further case for the intentional inclusion of educational experiences that foster imagination?

Fostering creativity and imagination in early childhood

Having skills in creativity and imagination can yield immense personal, educational, and professional gains. And if we want to help children develop these skills, research shows we should be allowing for repeated engagement with creative endeavors and materials (Kaufman & Gregoire, 2015). Fostering creativity requires setting up a classroom environment that inspires, invites wonder and expression, and is supported by positive relationships and planning that is flexible and responsive to the student's needs. I have seen this done very successfully in Reggio Emilia-inspired classrooms and elsewhere.

How do we foster creativity and imagination in our early childhood classrooms?

- Does the environment and display of materials encourage and inspire creative expression? If not, what changes can be made to the organization and placement of materials?
- Do my lessons invite wonder?

- Do I provide the time, space, and materials for children to express themselves creatively?
- Do I provide process-oriented and formative feedback on their creative endeavors that communicates high expectations?
- Do I challenge them to see things differently and extend their creative ideas and interests?
- What other materials or experiences can I provide to broaden their creativity and thinking?
- Does my pedagogy and curriculum invite the freedom to think deeply and differently?

Fostering creativity and careful observation through visual arts

Here are seven key principles of fostering creativity through art from Elliot Eisner:

1. The arts teach children that problems can have more than one solution and that questions can have more than one answer.

2. The arts celebrate multiple perspectives. There are many ways to see and interpret the world.

3. The arts teach children that in complex forms of problem solving, purposes are seldom fixed, but change with circumstances and opportunity. Learning the arts requires the ability and willingness to surrender to the unanticipated possibilities of the work as it unfolds.

4. The arts make vivid the fact that neither words in their literal form nor numbers exhaust what one can know. The limits of our language do not define the limits of our cognition.

5. The arts teach students that small differences can have large effects.

6. The arts teach students to think through and within a material.

7. The arts enable us to have experiences we can have from no other source, and, through such experiences, to discover the range and variety of what we are capable of feeling.

The visual arts help us to inspect our own ideas more carefully. In looking at, experiencing, and creating art, we train our minds to notice and consider that which would otherwise go unnoticed. Careful observation and looking at objects or phenomena from new angles are habits that are developed by good visual arts teachers.

In his book, *Art and the Creation of Mind*, Eisner makes a very interesting connection between perceiving subtleties and recognizing complexities. These two nuanced skills are necessary for differentiation. Differentiation, he argues, enables children to organize, categorize, and form concepts. It would make sense that children that practice noticing and recording subtle differences become better at both noticing and recording them. These differences become part of the child's understanding of that which is being observed and informs the overall schema they are creating about that particular category of 'things'. As children mature, we want to help them differentiate among qualitative attributes as they explore, create categories of phenomena, and make meaning. As children become better at observing subtleties, they are also becoming better at the skill of sustained attention and iteration. In making art, children often take a step back, look at their creations, and then add a color or a mark. Classrooms that have a practice of peer critique encourage members of the class to notice a subtle quality and explain it, or perhaps inspire further changes. This, of course, can happen while making any type of representational or abstract art form and in any art media.

Practice with careful observation involves many developing skills at once including the executive function skill of impulse control or inhibitory response. Above all, careful observation requires children to slow down. One cannot see subtle differences in color or shape, for example, if rushing to make and move on. Therefore, encouraging the careful observation of subtleties also gives children the opportunity to hone the executive function skill of focus. Once careful observation becomes a regular classroom event, it can become a habit – at that point it has the potential to become a skill that teaches itself. What I mean is, children can start to see for themselves how slowing down and controlling impulses helps them to create better artwork, art that they are more engaged in making and proud to share. This then becomes part of their own repertoire of skills.

Visual arts teach not only the *observation* of subtitles, but also the purposeful *creation* of subtleties. A practice that I have used for years in both preschool and kindergarten classrooms is having children regularly do observational drawings. Children have sketchbooks that are pulled out once a week at a designated time. While setting up this routine takes some time at the beginning of the school year, it quickly becomes a well-oiled machine. Children look at the object that the teacher has put out and decide where they will sit for their desired perspective. They quietly sit with their black felt tip pen to notice and record line and shape. Once they have done this, they focus on color, including tones and shadows, using colored pencils. This activity would be equally at home in a science class as in an art or homeroom one, the skills children are honing are useful across all disciplines.

The use of plentiful and varied materials

Fostering a culture of creativity means getting children comfortable with a variety of materials. Children have an innate drive to get their hands on materials and explore their characteristics. Each time a teacher introduces a new material, they are inviting the children to do two different exercises: to explore the new material's attributes and features, and second, to discover how it can be used in different ways. The teacher intentionally decides how much guidance to give and the right moments to give it. For example, before setting up a watercolor painting activity, I have the children gather around and watch how I use the paintbrushes, water, palette, paper towel, and paper. I don't do a lot of talking during the demonstration as I am asking them to focus on their observations. I then ask them what they noticed about how and when I used the water, the paper towel, etc. I ask questions like, 'what did you notice about the paint when I used less water? What did you notice when I used a smaller brush?' After collecting and discussing their observations, I fill in the essential information that they need to know before they get started on their own painting. After this initial period of guided instruction with the material, children begin to explore on their own. Using the same material for several days consecutively gives the children an opportunity to build upon the previous day's discoveries. I extend their exploration of the material by introducing other materials on which to use the watercolor. So, for example, if we began on watercolor paper, I would subsequently introduce other mediums such yupo paper or textured paper, which react very differently to the liquid nature of the paint. We would also paint on air dry clay and other objects that can take the paint. Depending on the interest and age of the children I am working with, I might return to a more guided instruction to demonstrate various techniques and reactions of the watercolor when combined with other art materials.

Exploration with a variety of art materials allows young children to build competence in:

- Investigating and drawing conclusions about the attributes and potential of those materials.
- Expressing themselves in non-discursive forms.
- Building focus and attention in self-initiated ideas.
- Gaining fine motor skills that transfer to other areas and tools in school.
- Building knowledge of how different materials can be used and making connections to how different materials are used by adults (for example, how wood, glass, metal, plastic, clay, etc. are used).
- Using their imagination in multiple ways (children often have stories that go along with their artistic creations).

Not all children will love using all materials and different materials will challenge their thinking and their skills in different ways. This is another reason why providing a large variety of materials is beneficial; all children will have moments of pride as well as moments of struggle.

I have already repeatedly referenced the Reggio Emilia Approach, and I would be remiss if I did not now mention a key concept from this approach: giving children '100 languages' to construct and express meaning. This refers to the idea of finding 100 ways to engage in the world of meaning making. It is tied to the core belief that children are communicators, and that one of our jobs as teachers is to foster their intellectual development through a systematic focus on symbolic representations. Such symbolic representations include words, but also other 'languages' such as movement, painting, drawing, building, sculpture, dramatic play, music, etc. It is a core belief in Reggio Emilia-inspired schools that children should not only be encouraged to use many materials, but that they have the *right* to do so. It is necessary in order for them to discover and communicate what they know, understand, wonder about, question, feel, and imagine. From this perspective, working with various art media provides much more than experience with those medias themselves, it provides essential ways of knowing, being, and experiencing the world.

The knowledge, understanding, and experience gained through years of exploring materials creatively and with imagination is not something that can or should disappear after early childhood. After kindergarten, incorporating frequent experiences with art materials becomes much harder for the teacher, as students' days get filled with more academically focused classes, lessons, and skills. However, the knowledge, understanding, and experiences created and used as those competencies were formed will carry through the neural networks they established. Associations of agency, pride, and joy were also likely formed by encounters with art in early years. And for those that still don't see the utility of understanding different materials later in life, think of what engineers do, or scientists, inventors, architects, manufacturers, and of course, artists. It is often through the creative use of materials that humans solve problems and present new ways of seeing and thinking.

To be excited by your own creative ideas

Me: What is your favorite book?

Leah: I don't know what my favorite book is yet because I have not *written* it yet! And I will make the drawings too! It will be a looooong series. And I will teach things … through my stories!

Leah, age five

This interaction that I had with one of my students happened recently and of course, it had my heart soaring. This is what we all want! We want our students to have the confidence and sense of self-efficacy to know that they are going to write and illustrate their favorite series. To be creative and excited about the potential of their imaginative ideas. And then to think about what they can teach through their stories – how they can connect with others and weave together ideas.

While this was a recent experience, over the 23 years that I have been teaching in early childhood classrooms, I have been amazed at how my students' imagination and creativity often goes beyond the limits of what I thought was possible. This is humbling and inspiring at the same time. It is why we cannot set the limits of a creative project, because doing so would assume that we are the most creative in the classroom. In early childhood classrooms, I have also witnessed how creativity and imagination can be contagious. I have seen how the ideas of one student can spark ideas in a peer in ways that I would not be able to as a teacher.

Summary

Creative thinking has always been and will always be, a central part of what makes life worth living. Life as a creative thinker can bring not only economic rewards, but also joy, fulfillment, purpose, and meaning. Children deserve nothing less.

Mitchel Resnick (2017)

If school is a place for learning, then it should also be a place for research and creativity. Encouraging children to represent and communicate their ideas and thoughts through the full range of symbolic systems should be one of the key elements in early childhood education. We need to adopt a 'can-do' approach and get creative about fostering creativity in our classrooms. We must *create* the conditions to inspire and challenge our students' endeavors while encouraging diverse experiences and the freedom to think deeply and differently. This is done by creating the physical environments, providing the tools and materials, as well as the meaningful opportunities for children to make mistakes, iterate, reflect, daydream, have autonomy in making creative decisions, find their purpose, express their unique perspectives and identities, and define personal goals. Creativity, imagination, and the arts should not simply be add-ons to the school day, but an intentional and integral part of one's experience at school. The opportunity to be creative in inspiring spaces activates learning as well as the disposition of mind that seeks further learning and creating.

Alignment to Practice

- Take time to look over the questions in the section entitled 'Fostering creativity and imagination in early childhood'. Reflect on them and address any areas for change and in your own practice. Discuss these potential changes or iterations with a colleague and collaborate on potential creative solutions.

- Provide opportunities for children to use plentiful and varied materials.

- Creativity takes time. Consider the amount of time children are being given to think and explore the properties of materials. How long do they get to consider their message and composition, make mistakes, and make iterations?

- Incorporate a practice of close observation. Explicitly demonstrate how an object can look different at a quick glance versus what nuances in color, detail, and line emerge with slow and careful observation.

- Give children ample opportunities to talk about their artwork. One method is to add a piece of acetate as an overlay to the artwork. The acetate contains the child's words, their thinking, descriptions, and labeling of their painting or drawing underneath. This can then be attached to one side of the artwork. Now you have not only documented their learning and creative work, but teachers, peers, and parents can either see the art on its own or with its explanatory gloss.

- Novelty is always intriguing to children so finding new materials or a new combination of materials is likely to gain their attention and elicit prolonged exploration.

- Regular practice.

- Encourage familiarity with the words imagine, create, wonder, and iterate.

Further reading

Eisner, Elliot W. (2002) *The Arts and the Creation of Mind.*

Hee Kim, Kyung (2018) *The Creativity Challenge: How we can recapture American Innovation.*

Magsaman, Susan and Ivy Ross (2023) *Your Brain on Art: How the Arts transform us.*

Resnick, Mitchel (2017) *Lifelong Kindergarten: Cultivating creativity through projects, passion, peers, and play.*

Kaufman, Scott Barry and Carolyn Gregoire (2015) *Wired to Create: Unraveling the mysteries of the creative mind.*

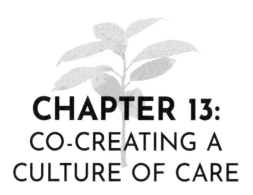

CHAPTER 13:
CO-CREATING A
CULTURE OF CARE

What is a culture of care?

A culture of care goes beyond thoughts and intentions. It is embodied in words and actions and is felt by every member of the community. A culture like this takes effort to sustain, is continuous, and seeks to embrace the diverse identities of its members.

This takes intellect, empathy, and compassion. Intellectually, our knowledge of the research on social cognition, emotion, and the science of belonging, helps us to plan, organize, and respond appropriately. Empathy is necessary to understand the feelings and perspectives of others. Compassion is when this empathy moves us to action. In a culture of care, one can show vulnerability and know it will be ok. In a culture of care, each voice matters and all can thrive.

Stress, challenges, and disappointments are part of everyday life for both children and the adults in their lives. But when we are connected to a supportive community that cares about who we are (not just what we can do), how we are feeling (even if those feelings are unpleasant), and our potential, we can face those stresses, challenges and disappointments. We can all learn from the fumbles and mistakes we face together. A culture of care fosters connection, resilience, and growth.

Diversity, equity, and belonging

> Belonging may be as essential to the mind as breathing is to the body.

> Daniel J. Siegel (2020)

A central theme of this book is that our emotional and social well-being is essential to brain development, learning, and thriving in school and beyond. As social mammals, our social networks have been the bedrock of our survival. It is the story of humanity. We need each other for basic survival, but we also need each other for healthy brain development. The longest scientific study of happiness ever conducted – The Grant Study – makes it quite clear that being a part of a supportive community is the most important factor associated with health, happiness, and longevity. We feel a sense of belonging when we are a valued member of a community to which we also contribute. All humans need this sense of belonging just like we need oxygen to breathe.

While trends have risen and fallen, more schools and businesses are taking diversity, equity, and inclusion or belonging more seriously than they have in the past. There are more conferences, graduate programs, official positions of employment, books, and articles to broaden discussion and increase awareness and strategic change of these issues. Granted, not all efforts have been authentic or successful, but some are on their way and improving the lives of children, families, teachers, and whole communities. However, without *care*, diversity, equity, and inclusion is just an intellectual exercise. If we care, we try harder to understand another's perspective, we design and re-design to address the complexities of positive identity formation in today's world, and we act for the benefit of the valued individual and our community as a whole.

When we talk about a culture of care and belonging in a school or classroom, it should include every student and teacher as well as all the other adults in the building. That is, everyone needs to show care *and* feel cared for. In this chapter, I will bring together concepts already discussed in previous chapters related to learning and well-being, and show how they connect to support a culture of care.

Identity

A child's experiences at school affect their identity as a person and as a learner. This multi-dimensional understanding of self is constantly evolving according to academic, social, and cultural realities (Osher, et al, 2020). Identity is closely tied to self-efficacy – belief in one's potential – and this 'can have profound effects on their academic engagement, and in turn their growth trajectory' (Gotlieb, et al, 2022). Returning once again to the concept of dispositions of mind, we want children to self-identify as people who seek understanding and connection and who see themselves as valuable contributors to the learning community. Caring for a child means caring for the different dimensions of their identity and knowing that all contribute to a certain disposition of mind, success, and well-being both in and out of school.

Relationships

> Relationship is the primary connecting dimension of our system, however, understood not merely as a warm, protective envelope, but rather as a dynamic conjunction of forces and elements interacting toward a common purpose.
>
> Loris Malaguzzi (quoted in Edwards, et al, 1998)

Relationships are at the heart of education and a culture of care, both symbolically and in real life. This is because they are the precursors for engagement and thriving for children and adults. Identity formation, disposition of mind towards learning, competency development, mastery of domain-specific knowledge, motivation, higher-order problem-solving skills, and ultimately, academic achievement all depend upon and are heavily influenced by relationships. We want our relationships to be growing and strengthening as the school year progresses and therefore this mutually beneficial condition needs to be continuously fostered. This effort requires intentional check-ins with ourselves and the individuals we work with (both children and adults) and a desire to understand how someone is feeling and why they are feeling that way. It requires proactive design, which is why incorporating relationship-building games and activities into the school day should not be seen as a detractor from learning but rather as a means for elevating learning and thriving.

Building Community

A useful definition of community is one that I borrow from author Charles H. Vogl, 'a group of individuals who share a mutual concern for one another's welfare'. This message is simple yet profound if we reflect on our classroom and school communities. How visible is our mutual concern for each other's welfare? Is it felt? Is it felt by all? The communities of which we are a part are our social worlds. As such, they have enormous impact on the way we feel and show up in the world, and this can be in negative or positive ways. This applies to not only the children, but the teachers as well and the two influence each other.

In communities that are imbued by a culture of care, members hold each other accountable for how they show care. They are places where children are taught to care explicitly and implicitly (through adult modeling). They are places where children necessarily practice their own skills of caring. Social norms emerge in preschool as their egocentrism wanes, and they begin to understand the meaning and value of a social contract among peers. Micheal Tomasello explains that even young children have a sense of shared intentionality, a strong sense of 'we'. The socialization that happens when children are young, helps them to understand the benefits of reciprocity, the value of connection and belonging, as well as the discomfort of a lack of belonging.

Agency

All people – and I mean scholars, researchers, and teachers, who in any place have set themselves to study children seriously – have ended up by discovering not so much the limits and weaknesses of children but rather their surprising and extraordinary strengths and capabilities linked with an inexhaustible need for expression and realization.

Loris Malaguzzi (quoted in Edwards, et al, 1998)

The theme of agency comes up frequently in this book and overlaps with many MBE concepts. When teachers use agency-supportive practices, like providing choice and creating forums for children's voice, they tap into an innate human psychological need for autonomy which aids well-being, motivation, and engagement. Agency is necessary for a sense of

self-efficacy and the disposition of mind that we are trying to
As part of most successful learning processes, we need to h
in time for discovery, trying things out, and coming up with our own
connections and ideas, alongside instruction. Part of showing care is
intentionally giving children a sense of agency, and part of feeling cared
for as teachers is being allowed to feel the reward of our own efforts,
intelligence, activity, and energy. As previously stated, self-belief is a key
predictor for both educational outcomes and life successes.

Teaching caring is showing caring and vice versa

Care needs are an essential ingredient of the classroom environment
(both physical and felt), but they should also be thought of as a key part
of our curriculum and pedagogy.

Young children learn from everything we say and do so naturally, when
we show caring, children learn about caring. We show care in small
mundane ways through eye contact, emotional check-ins, scaffolding
with patience, active listening, and assisting children when in the throes
of big emotions or social conflicts. For younger children, we show
caring in how we assist in their daily rituals of staying sanitary, sharing
meals, and managing clothing. We can also show care by creating and
sustaining a practice of classroom conversations in which we address
each other by name, and by making space for everyone to express
themselves, verbally and/or non-verbally. Demonstrating that we care
means reminding children continuously that their feelings matter, just
as much as their ideas, questions, and physical and mental well-being.

From helping children wash their hands or escorting them to the nurse,
to asking them what they think or feel in a conversation, to the bigger
picture ways like researching new ways of building upon their interests
in a long-term project, the teacher/researcher shows, teaches, and models
care.

A word about teacher well-being and burnout

I have tried to make the teacher-learner present as much as possible while
discussing MBE concepts. Anyone with a brain is a learner and thus

subject to all the topics of this book. As I said earlier, teachers matter. Period. They matter because they are human beings and members of the community. And, yes, they absolutely matter in how they affect the children. It is imperative, therefore, that we in the field of education consider teacher well-being and this means addressing their sense of belonging, their work/life balance, and their growth as professionals and humans. Teaching is inherently intense work that requires much thought, effort, hard work, emotional intelligence, and patience. It is endlessly rewarding. It can also be very stressful.

When teacher well-being is not addressed, a number of undesirable outcomes are possible, one of them being teacher burnout. Burnout is often the result of a toxic work environment and it arises when stress outpaces our ability to cope and/or when the root causes seem entirely out of our control. Work/life balance and giving teachers agency can be protectors from this type of stress. Since the beginning of the Covid 19 pandemic in 2020, many people have been concerned about teacher burnout and for good reason. But even before the pandemic in 2017, Yale's Center for Emotional Intelligence in collaboration with The New Teacher Center found that 70% of the five thousand teachers that they surveyed reported that much of their day involves feeling stressed, overwhelmed, and frustrated (Brackett, 2019).

Building supportive communities in which teachers feel known, supported, and inspired just as we want students to be known, supported, and inspired is a job for all members of the school community. What actionable steps can leaders make in this important effort? What actionable steps can individual teachers make? Addressing teacher belonging is a first step. Honoring teacher's time and work/life balance has to be prioritized. Allowing for agency and support in their professional and individual growth, and going back to the chapter on teacher/researchers, incorporating systems that support sustaining collaborations among teachers are all impactful endeavors. Teachers are less likely to feel burnout or leave when they work in a supportive community. Let's consider all of the brains – and all of the humans – in the school building so that we all feel cared for and can all thrive.

Summary

A culture of caring is a fertile ground in which we can all learn and grow. It requires continuous tending to make sure that all of our members feel cared for. We show care with intellect, empathy, and compassion. This goes beyond intentions and should be seen and felt by all members of the school. A sense of belonging should be pervasive, like oxygen, and it needs to be central to our thinking, and overlap with all other aspects of our pedagogy and curriculum. A culture of care takes the individual seriously: it values their positive identity formation, associations with school and teachers, and ideas and interests, and gives them opportunities to exercise agency and develop self-efficacy. It also takes the community's needs seriously, and values coming together, connection between individuals, and rewarding relationships that engender growth.

Buttressed by a caring and supportive community that values our welfare as humans, we can develop our individual and collective sense of self-efficacy and we can grow together.

Alignment to Practice

- Create buddy systems with other classes and grades.
- Create opportunities for children to build relationships with non-faculty adults in the building. Can we use this as an opportunity to show our appreciation for the work they do?
- Help the children form relationships with other community organizations.
- Model acts of caring and narrate those observed among students and adults.

Further reading

Hammond, Zaretta. (2015) *Culturally Responsive Teaching And The Brain: Promoting authentic engagement and rigor among culturally and linguistically diverse students.*

Siegel, Daniel J. (2022) *The Developing Mind: How relationships and the brain interact to shape who we are.*

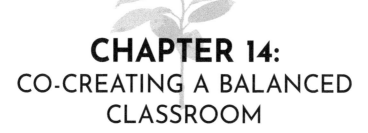

CHAPTER 14:
CO-CREATING A BALANCED CLASSROOM

I'd like to start this chapter by addressing a couple of pervasive but counterproductive dichotomies that divide educators and ways of thinking in unhelpful ways and prevent us from creating a balanced classroom.

Unhelpful dichotomies

Traditional versus progressive

I am one of the many teachers out there who see the merits of practices that are associated with both traditional and progressive education. We don't have to claim one over the other – that is what makes this dichotomy unhelpful. As teacher/researchers we should be open to what the science of learning says, as well as what we know from our professional experience. Let's take what works and use them both. Traditional versus progressive might be the biggest dichotomy that exists in the field of education, but it is not the only one. In fact, I am sure that the ones below will sound familiar as well.

The reading divide (aka the reading war)

While there is much nuance to both sides of this argument, in its simplest terms, the reading divide is the impassioned disagreement between those that believe that prioritizing systematic phonics is how we should teach children how to read and those that believe in prioritizing whole language. I remember when I first heard the term, 'the reading wars,' I thought to myself, 'do we really need to be so dramatic?' Well, words are powerful. When two approaches become staunchly entrenched camps then people end up getting heated. A difference of perspective and experience can become 'war', with both sides claiming their approach is based on research and that the other side is harming students. Newer teachers often end up choosing the 'side' that their school is already on. The divide continues. Let me ask you something? In war, do humans calmly listen to the other side and have productive conversations about what each side has in common? So ... maybe the word 'war' should be abandoned. If nothing else, educators should always have the interests of the children in common. Both sides could use some humility and acknowledge a level of uncertainty while maintaining their beliefs.

Instructional approaches to literacy maintain their scientific credibility by the systematic search for answers along with an openness to consider what factors might have been missed, what might be improved, what might have even greater impact, and what unintentional side effects might occur. Literacy is a right for all children. It affects many aspects of a child's growth and development and is tied to success in all subject areas and life beyond school. Literacy is also complex! It is a mega-skill that encompasses many distinct skills. It makes sense that there is a multitude of passionate opinions on how to best go about teaching it.

As should be clear from the subjects and positions I take in this book, I follow promising research in the science of reading, and it informs how I teach. I have Hollis Scarborough's Reading Rope – a graphic illustrating the 'weave' between word recognition and language comprehension – by my desk to remind me of all the strands of skills (and corresponding research) that need to be considered and addressed by a robust literacy program. There is no question that comprehensive and explicit phonics instruction is necessary to build the neural networks for decoding. However, we can also agree that deep reading and strong literacy skills and dispositions require attention to student motivation and social-emotional functioning (Gotlieb, et al, 2022). Furthermore, literacy is supported by an understanding of grammar and narrative arcs, the power of words to move and inspire, and the development of rich background knowledge (Willingham, 2017).

We all need to be open to incorporating new research and perspectives, for the chances are that the science of reading will continue to evolve and suggest changes to practice. Claude Goldenberg (2021) states,

> The unknowns around the science of reading are rarely acknowledged adequately by reading-science advocates. This can give the 'science' part of the 'science of reading' a bad name.

Let's honor science and our knowledge and experience at the same time by continuously learning from research and each other without taking sides in a 'war'. Let's respectfully engage in dialogue with a spirit of empathy and intellectual curiosity if for no other reason than to increase understanding all around. This approach, which I would argue is being a teacher/researcher, enables us to be nimble, and to act quickly to correct mistakes. We want children to be flexible and learn from mistakes. We too need to be flexible and learn from our own.

Freedom versus structure

For some, the idea of freedom in classrooms looks and feels like chaos and they worry that the result is a lack of focus on necessary content or skills. On the other side, many educators shiver at the very thought of a structured classroom as a draconian or factory-like model. However, an effective and intentional classroom should have both freedom and structure, so let's think about what that balance could look like. Designing classrooms and curricula for student choice and opportunities for play does not necessitate a removal of structure. Students need structure (clear objectives, organized materials, clear behavioral expectations, informative feedback, scaffolding, etc.) but all of that can be done while supporting student agency. And this dichotomy is not specific to early childhood educators. Those in higher education, like Jose Antonio Bowen, also strive for balance here: 'Just as organizations and societies must balance freedom with control, and safety with cost, educators must live in the tension between needing to teach the same content or process to each student while wanting also to increase the potential and capacities of individual people in unique ways.' (Bowen, 2021).

Master teachers know that there is still a structure in creating the learning experience and scaffolding, supporting, and documenting the learning.

There is structure in how the teacher then takes the data from a day to plan for the next. They ask themselves, 'What foundational knowledge and skills are necessary? What key knowledge is needed for the children to take their learning to the next level?' Teachers will front load content at the beginning of a project, for example, teaching children about important architects and concepts of architecture before embarking on a project in designing their own school. Or making sure the children grasp concepts in numeracy and simple equations before asking them to design a board game with a numberpath. A gap in conceptual understanding may arise during a project, and the attentive and intentional teacher will interrupt the project to address this gap. In a balanced classroom, students feel the safety of structure because they know their teacher is intentionally providing learning opportunities, monitoring logistics, and making adjustments based on their observations and judgements. But students also feel the joy of being curious, creative, collaborative, and constructive themselves.

One of my favorite aspects of teaching is discovering what amazing things children can create when given the opportunity. Early in my career while teaching at Bing Nursery School, I remember being in complete awe of the direction a five-year-old student took a project idea. I had set up a small center of various art materials designed to encourage the use of multiple media. Students could make anything they wanted. One child quietly went to work and purposefully used every material available in the creation of a 20-inch robot with movable joints. He manipulated two-dimensional construction paper to make three-dimensional limbs, a torso, head, hands, and feet that he attached with wire. He was intent on having the robot move like a human, but he was also intent on having it look 'cool' with the use of color and detail. He used markers and colored pencils to add texture, buttons, and facial features. I would have never imagined that a child would have created such a masterpiece when I set out the materials. This was the first time I witnessed the power of providing freedom and choice, but it has not been the last!

Joy versus rigor

I have heard Robert Kosasky, Head of St. Andrew's Episcopal School in Potomac, Maryland, say, 'Parents do not have to choose, teachers do not have to choose, and children certainly do not have to choose; we can and should design for both [joy and rigor]!'

We are aiming for balance. We are trying to be informed by and knowledgeable about all of the different strategies, techniques, and learning experiences that contribute to healthy, thriving, engaged learners. We are doing our best to stay abreast of MBE research, where the indices point, and how to increase and elevate learning that is both rigorous and rewarding. Shouldn't we then be intellectually curious ourselves, and think deeply and creatively to balance all these factors in learning experiences that both teach and inspire?

Co-creating a balanced classroom

Focusing alone on the cognitive facets of achievements in language, mathematics, or science is insufficient because context – relationships, environments, and experiences – provides the energy that drives the brain's electrical circuitry and develops the neural pathways that build increasingly complex skills.

Cantor, et al (2021)

To co-create a classroom (or a school) that encompasses all of the research on optimal learning and development for young children is an exercise in finding balance. With so many aspects considered essential, how does one even begin to aim for balance between them? The answer is definitely not to make the school day longer. And, unfortunately, there is no neat formula that can be applied across all schools. Individual institutions are naturally going to have different philosophies, mission statements, and cultures. However, as Cantor points out, all of these pieces are necessary in order for children to build the neural pathways and complex skills that are needed for them to live successful lives. In this chapter, I am going to synthesize the ideas and research presented in this book to help you address what a balance could look like in your school or classroom.

Let's begin with your philosophy and goals. Schools usually have well-crafted and inspirational mission statements. If you had to describe *your own* goals in education, what would they be? A connected – though potentially different – question is, what is the purpose of early childhood education? Put this book down for a minute and formulate an answer to these questions. This reflective exercise is a necessary precedent of finding balance. If two people have differing ideas about the goals and purposes of early childhood education, they are likely to arrive at divergent answers about what constitutes 'balance', even if they are informed by the same research.

> Write here:

These goals will be key for you when you try to apply the framework for balance presented below, in your own context and practice.

Goals, purpose, and balance

In 2022, a study was published that shook up many in the world of education, especially early childhood education. Some were surprised. Others found their beliefs and experiences to be reaffirmed. The findings showed that a statewide public pre-k program taught by licensed teachers had a measurable and statistically significant *negative* effect on learning, achievement, and behavior for the children in the study. Let's look at why.

In a study that lasted over a decade, Dale Farran and colleagues looked at the impact of pre-kindergarten programs on 2,990 low-income children in Tennessee. Of these children, some were admitted to pre-kindergarten by lottery and others were rejected. This situation created a perfect opportunity for Farran to measure impact by comparing student achievement between the two groups over a period of years, a conveniently randomized, controlled trial. The students were followed up until middle school. At the end of the first year, the children that went to pre-kindergarten scored higher on school readiness measures. Here comes the surprise to many (but not all). After third grade, the children who went to pre-kindergarten started performing worse than the control group. In what ways? They had lower test scores, they were more likely to get into trouble at school (including suspensions), and were more likely to be placed in special education programs. By 6th grade, these same children had continued their downward slide as represented in their math, science, and reading scores.

This study does not prove that preschool is bad for children; other studies have shown how preschool has contributed to learning and achievement gains over time. So, what went wrong in Tennessee? What was it about their preschool program that created a small win at the beginning but then a long and comprehensive decline in student success? Farran has some ideas about what was going wrong, and her thoughts are consistent with MBE research and the ideas expressed in this book. She conjectures that due to the unreasonable expectations of this overly academic preschool experience, where children were very much controlled by adults, these children were not learning self-regulation skills. In fact, Farran thought she might even have been witnessing 'an almost allergic reaction to the amount of external control that they're having to experience in school'. The big takeaway, in Farran's own words is:

> Ideally, pre-K should involve more play, with teachers interacting with students and encouraging them to explore their interests.

Farran's worry is that preschool lacks balance. There is too much whole-group instruction. Behavioral control is too rigid. There is not enough time side. And there is too much time in which teachers are talking, instead of listening (Farran, 2022; Mader, 2022; Kamenetz, 2022).

I am now going to present a conceptual framework for balance, one that considers the integrated developmental story of the individual student. As a conceptual framework, it is intentionally general rather than specific. There is space for educators and school leaders to specify their own thoughts and goals in respect to balance as they consider *their* community of learners.

A framework for balance in early childhood education

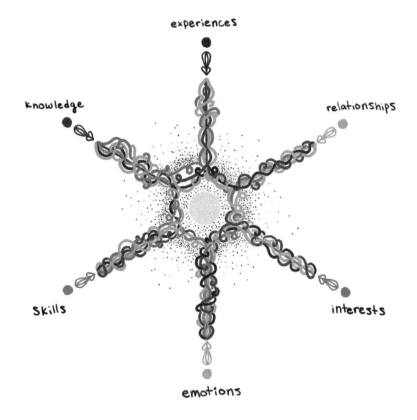

Experiences, relationships, knowledge, skills, interests, and emotions

How much of your class time is dedicated to knowledge building? Do you spend a lot of time teaching skills? What about relationship-building? Every once in a while, it is good to analyze your plan for the week to make sure it gives adequate time to all of these crucial elements for optimal learning. An iteration might be required. Remember, children are more likely to successfully build knowledge and skills if their classroom experiences are engaging, the lessons hold meaning for *them*, the emotions in the room are positive, and their relationships are strong. There is an intricate connection between emotion to cognition: feeling and thinking, thinking and feeling, go together. Oftentimes, in early childhood classrooms, we can provide experiences that help to develop relationships, knowledge, and skills simultaneously.

Diverse nutrients

Earlier in the book, I shared Dr. Kim's theory that children require 'diversity in their soil' to grow curious and creative minds. Another analogy is that of a toolbox. We want children to have a collection of tools, each representing a different way of solving a problem. Each skill or area of knowledge offers a way of seeing a problem from a different angle; it provides an alternate approach to solving problems and creating understanding. In terms of neuroanatomy, we want to help children build robust neural networks, and therefore to make many connections through different disciplines and modalities. Buttressed by strong relationships, balance is achieved when children are exposed to a diversity of learning experiences and skill development, all informing an overall understanding of the world around them (and their role in it). Many will overlap, but this range should include experiences with:

- Disciplines including the sciences, social studies, languages, and mathematics.

- Community building activities that support belonging and social-cognitive skills.

- Lessons and activities designed to help develop emotional intelligence.

ual arts for the unique ways they help children see, understand,
te, and communicate meaning and identity.

- Performing arts for the unique ways they help children see, understand, create, and communicate meaning and identity.
- A diversity of cultural exposure, perspectives, and experiences.
- Physical activities that are playful and joyous.
- Exploring the natural world both inside and outside the classroom.
- Rest to aid consolidation of learning and well-being.
- Reflection to aid with meta-cognition.

Direct Instruction and Other Learning Experiences

Direct instruction has been mentioned a few times in this book as a pedagogical approach that has a positive impact on academic outcomes in the right situations, at the right ages, and in the right doses. The total absence of direct instruction leads to problems just as surely as too much will. Without any, classrooms can lack the structure and routines needed for children to feel that they are part of a safe and predictable environment. A level of structure and routine allows for teacher observation, guidance, and scaffolding. The right amount of direct instruction allows children to feel a sense of self-efficacy for they receive that little burst of dopamine when they can see the progress they are making on a certain skill. Additionally, direct instruction is especially impactful for older children and in certain subject areas. Explicit and systematic instruction is not just useful, but necessary, when learning how to read, write, and understand various math concepts. In fact, in the case of the science of reading, after years of debate there is consensus among researchers and teachers alike that teaching phonological awareness and phonics ought to be done through an explicit, systematic, repetitive, and multi-sensory approach to help build the complicated neural networks needed to lift words off a page.

Reading skills including vocabulary, comprehension, writing, and fluency, also all benefit from explicit and systematic instruction. However, studies have shown that direct instruction in the early years of schooling can backfire by making children 'less curious, less likely to discover new information, and less likely to make new, unexpected connections' (Kaufman & Gregoire, 2015; Gopnik, 2011). As Immordino-Yang, Darling-Hammond, and Krone (2018), put it:

> True, it is important to enable students to learn symbol systems that help organize the brain for academic skills. However, it is also true that the very processes of reasoning, conversing, exploring and conjecturing strengthen the coherence and balance of brain networks, fostering greater intelligence to apply to all kinds of learning tasks.

While there is a place for direct instruction – more so in kindergarten than in preschool – there is also the danger of too much. If too much of the children's school day is being given to the explicit direction and task-oriented activities, what are they pushing out?

Children need time and intentional care for relationships to form, between students and teachers as well as with their peers. They need time to wonder, discover, create, make their own new connections, and ask their own questions. They need the time to play.

Earlier, I wrote that a level of direct instruction can assist with teacher observations, guidance, and scaffolding. However, observations, guidance, and scaffolding may not be possible if children are not afforded open-ended exploration or play. Observing and documenting children during open-ended learning experiences gives the teacher invaluable information about how each child seeks to find meaning, where they might be struggling, and what they find interesting. Too much direct instruction can inhibit children from practicing and developing confidence in expressing themselves,

What is the right amount of direct instruction? It will vary as class dynamics and ages vary, but whatever the amount, it needs to be balanced by intentional opportunities for downtime, creativity, exploration and discovery, and socialization. Balanced and productive early childhood programs are intentionally designed and iterated to offer rich environments and learning experiences that allow children to build a variety of skills including the opportunity to do so through pursuing their individual interests.

Types of play

There is increasing evidence that free and guided play contribute differently to different developmental outcomes (Pyle, 2018). Whereas free play is largely associated with the development of children's social and other generalized cognitive abilities such as creative problem-solving and self-regulation, guided play is associated with the acquisition of academic skills. All three categories of play (free, mutually directed, and guided) should be thoughtfully incorporated into early childhood education.

The teacher/researcher

The teacher/researcher never stops learning from MBE as well as other contributing disciplines like the arts. Successful and inspired learning communities are more possible if we ourselves are open to learning and iterating to improve upon our background knowledge and experience. This type of learning community needs to be supported by the leadership and administrative team as well as our teaching colleagues. School leaders will make some curricular and pedagogical decisions that impact teachers, but these can be balanced when teachers have a greater sense of agency, purpose, and creative input. Taken together, this balance supports teacher and student well-being while increasing the knowledge and skills teachers need to flexibly support student learning.

Flexibility

Balance is an ever-moving target when considering the complexity of teaching, learning, and individual people within their individual contexts. Therefore, we must stay open and flexible to necessary iterations as advances in the science of learning happen as well as our understanding of our own learners changes or become more apparent.

Early childhood teachers are balancing a similar yet different set of needs to teachers of older grades. They need to provide warm and predictable routines and environments while simultaneously giving children ample opportunities to pursue their curiosity, to explore, and play. Flexibility *has to* be part of the plan. Iterating on the spot should be expected. Early childhood educators need to be *opportunists*, to use their background knowledge in child development and MBE to creatively respond to children's needs and burgeoning interests. And do this while promoting foundational skills, knowledge, positive associations with school, and dispositions of mind that students can carry with them for future learning.

The logistics of balance

Time limits and packed schedules

Most things that matter in early childhood development and education take time. So, time must be set aside for what matters. It takes time to develop relationships with children, relationships built on trust and shared respect and responsibility. It takes time to observe and document children's actions, to find and take advantage of those pivotal moments that spark a project or learning opportunity. It takes time to have meaningful conversations and give children the space to think and articulate their thoughts without feeling rushed. Exploring materials, making iterations to one's work, and active reflections take a lot of time. Building friendships and collaborative projects also takes time. Teacher guides and curricula plan books are several inches thick, and these lesson plans could fill each minute of every day of the school year without leaving time for much else. This is why we need to approach schedules in a balanced, intelligent, and intentional way while remaining open and flexible to make necessary adjustments. Being an intentional teacher/ researcher requires making choices that allocate time for students to be fully supported in the ways we have discussed while also allocating time for teachers to plan, consider alternatives, and iterate in order to address needs and opportunities.

What about assessment?

Different forms of assessment will be appropriate for different skills and purposes. For example, an assessment of a child's grasp of phonics is going to look a lot more uniform and prescribed than that of the same child's social cognitive skills. For all assessments, however, the goal should be to measure how a child is growing and learning compared to their previous abilities and competencies. While this goal seems obvious, it should be restated and reflected upon regularly for it is common

use assessments to compare children to one another or to
\o is the brightest in the classroom. While this data may be
useful at times, it is a big distraction from what school is supposed to
be about: the learning and growth trajectory of each individual student.

Assessment is also often used in the context of 'evidence-based' practices.
That is to say, we look to assessments to provide evidence of student
learning on the individual level, but we also use assessments to validate
a particular strategy or approach. Evidence is important and should
inform our pedagogical and curricular decisions. However, we have to
do better than just focus on quantitative evidence. I agree with Mitchel
Resnick (2017):

> [W]e need to broaden our view of evidence. Rather than just
> trying to *measure* what children learn (through numbers), we
> also need to *document* what children learn (through compelling
> examples).

For assessment to describe how a child has grown and how best to
support their further learning, there has to be a system of documentation.
Examples of what children did and how they felt during a lesson, whether
they were motivated in pursuit of a project idea or activity, how they
responded to a challenge, and what questions they posed, all provide
qualitative evidence that document children's learning and help teachers
give valuable feedback. Qualitative and quantitative evidence together
give us a better and more balanced story of a child's current level of
understanding as well as how to maximize their potential for future
growth.

Assessment should be treated as a process rather than just a file of
papers with a child's name on it. The majority of assessments (especially
in preschool) should be integrated into the learning experiences
themselves. Due to the subjective nature of assessment, teachers need
to be open to considering alternative hypotheses and different factors
that can be influencing a child's behavior, and this should also be part
of the documentation. Many schools have adopted the idea of 'authentic
assessment' through a more qualitative, consistent, and comprehensive
observation of day-to-day child activity. This type of assessment, linked
to measures, is culturally responsive and looks at the application of skills

and knowledge while the child is engaging in play or other activities. The teacher/researcher creates and sustains balanced assessment for each student, using both quantitative and qualitative data, which is continuous, rather than just consisting of progress reports or parent/ teacher conferences.

What we create time for and what we assess tells the world what we value in both implicit and explicit ways. If we truly care about student well- being, creativity, curiosity, motivation, knowledge, and skills, we need to create systems of assessment that focus on and represent these values, even if some aspects are just harder to measure than others.

Skills, experiences, and disposition of mind

According to *Quality Early Learning* – a report put out by The World Bank Group (Bendini & Devercelli, 2022) – preschool and the early grades have the ability to promote the development of the skills, knowledge, and attitudes that will enable children to thrive both in their schooling and in life:

> The real strength of high-quality ECE [early childhood education] is more commonly not the formal curriculum but the nature and quality of the relationships between the educators and the children.

It is, however, not just about relationships. According to the report there are three other key elements that are associated with children's long-term academic success and emotional well-being and those are 1) practices that support communication skills, 2) practices that support self-regulation (including emotional intelligence and regulation), and 3) practices that support active learning through play.

How does this relate back to disposition of mind? Well, a disposition of mind is how one *feels* about thinking and learning. A positive disposition can fuel an enduring motivation to keep on learning, thinking, and broadening or deepening one's understanding. Learning experiences which support a child's sense of autonomy, self-efficacy (sense of competence), and of self-worth (identity validation and a sense of belonging) enhance their development as powerful and self-motivated learners. Balanced early childhood programs don't lose sight of each of these important factors that impact learners now and in the future.

Summary

We aim for balance as we consider all the important aspects of learning, well-being, and brain development in early childhood classrooms. Before we can set out towards this goal, we need to be reflective and intentional about the aims of early childhood education; what constitutes 'balance', will diverge between educators if their ideas differ, even if those ideas are based on the same research. This chapter provides a conceptual framework that synthesizes ideas and research to promote a balance of experiences, relationships, knowledge, approaches, and skills in the classroom. It advocates a balance between direct instruction and exploratory learning, different types of playful learning, and between flexibility and sustainability in the teacher/researcher's own approach, workload, and context. Scheduling (what we make time for) and assessment (how and what we measure) tells the world in both implicit and explicit ways what we value. If we truly care about student well-being, creativity, curiosity, motivation, knowledge, and skills, we need to create schedules and systems of assessment that focus on and represent these values. Balance is an ever-moving target when considering the complexity of teaching, learning, and individual people within their individual contexts. Therefore, we must stay open and flexible to necessary iterations as advances in the science of learning happen and our understanding of our own learners changes or becomes more apparent.

Why not aspire to make our classroom and school loveable: a place for research, for re-cognition and reflection, a place where children, teachers and families learn and feel well?

Further reading

Christakis, Erika (2016)*The Importance of being little: What preschoolers really need from grownups*.

CHAPTER 15:
CONCLUSION

The research worker remains a student all [their] life. Preparation for [their] work is never finished for [they have] to keep abreast with the growth of knowledge ... this study becomes a habit and forms a regular part of the scientist's life.

W. I. B. Beveridge (1957)

It is commonly believed that childhood is a special period in life, meant to be marked by raucous joy and play, exploration and growth, burgeoning friendships, and close bonds to adults who show and model care. From an MBE perspective, early childhood is also a pivotal period of whole child development. As teachers, it is both an honor and a tremendous responsibility to play a role in an individual's childhood, a time in life in which beginnings are being created and nurtured. Our mission includes but goes beyond educational goals and academic benchmarks. We want to help children develop as human beings with enduring dispositions of mind that foster continuous understanding of the self and others and help them to find purpose and success.

Children's learning involves the gradual internalization of patterns, associations, procedures, and beliefs. Creating these deliberate and intentional experiences and relationships in schools helps to define how the child sees themself as a learner, how they view school, and the kind of thinking habits they will develop. This, in turn, influences the kind of cognitive skills they acquire. Beginnings don't just matter in the beginning. They matter for everything that comes next.

In this book we have spent time understanding structures of the brain and brain development as well as how neurons and neural networks grow and strengthen. We have looked at the special period in one's life called early childhood from an anthropological perspective, a psychological perspective, a neurological perspective, and an educational perspective. I would argue that throughout this book, we also look at the early childhood period from a *human* perspective, that is, we have considered elements of well-being, purpose, joy, global impact, and the future of the individual and the collective.

The role of teacher/researcher can impact children *and* teachers in a myriad of positive ways. Teaching is both a science and an art. To strive for a high level of impact, for a high level of knowledge, skills, and artistry, we have to embrace this role. The promotion of mastery in teaching is much more likely to be realized by continuous questioning and study than by employing formulas. It is through establishing strong relationships with the people in the school, research (both academic research and classroom processes of reflection and iteration), metacognition (thinking about our own thinking, goals, and intentions), and imagination (asking, 'how might I make this even better?') that we can best attain a level of true mastery.

We have focused on the value of play, emotion and cognition, social-cognitive skills, the power of classroom conversations, the role of creativity and the imagination, a culture of care, and what it means to strive for balance. Literacy and numeracy, two areas of curriculum that typically get the bulk of attention in the world of education, have been discussed as important areas of growth couched within the framework of balanced learning experiences supported by the other MBE inspired topics. Each chapter deep dive contributes to our overall aim of building children's repertoires of knowledge, skills, and behaviors to be ever more sophisticated, flexible, and creative while tending to their interests, sense of purpose, and self-efficacy.

Each discipline that we attend to professionally provides another perspective, another schema, through which we can better understand our role as a teacher and how best to relate to and support our students. Drawing on a variety of sources of expertise develops our own knowledge, building up the myelin and neural networks in our brains. There is an obvious parallel between our professional development and what is happening in our students' brains as they experience education. Each discipline at school – the visual arts, music, the sciences, history, social studies, foreign languages, literacy, numeracy, etc. – provides another perspective, another schema through which the world is organized and understood by the child, and entry points to find their own strengths and passions.

I have invited the reader to reflect on their own beliefs as they digest this information because beliefs matter. If we want children to have a strong practice in metacognition, then we need to have one ourselves. This means that we should take time, even in the midst of our hectic days, to ask ourselves what beliefs we hold about learning and early childhood education. Our beliefs and practices should be seamlessly integrated and part of a cohesive system.

This brings me to teaching with intention: to understand what is actually happening in the brains of our students; to stay abreast of MBE research that could have an impact; to actively think about and translate those findings into practice; to pay close attention to the needs, interests, and wonderings of the students; and to continuously design and iterate educational experiences that highlight their strengths and address weaknesses. Hopefully, the teacher/researcher also has the intention to support their colleagues in their roles and the collective goal of thinking creatively and intelligently about helping children learn and grow.

Teaching with intention also means taking the power of play seriously and paying attention to the relationship between cognition and emotion as well as the importance of social interactions and social cognition. It means thoughtfully considering what strategies or combinations of strategies help children most and in what circumstances; it is always striving for balance, so that children are being challenged academically, but also developing as well-rounded citizens of the world that have a sense of self-efficacy. Young children are little researchers with intellectual curiosity and enormous capacity to create and imagine. This is what makes early childhood such a special period in life and such a powerful age in which to teach and learn from children. Teaching with intention means holding and protecting this truth and letting it guide curricula and the design of environments and opportunities. Teaching with intention is simultaneously teaching with care. Caring for the development of the whole child and making sure that children feel that we care. These intentional practices foster and preserve a disposition of mind in each student that sees school as a place where they can be heard, understood, encouraged, challenged appropriately, and most importantly, sees learning as a life-long and endlessly valuable endeavor.

To bring all this knowledge and intention to bear we have to create a tapestry-like alignment of our practice and how we see our role; synthesizing the what, the why, and the how together. It sounds quite complicated, but that is also what makes it interesting and worth doing.

At the beginning of this book, I described the disposition of mind of a learner who is energized by their own level of intellectual curiosity, creativity, and care for others and the world. Seeking knowledge, understanding, and diverse perspectives while considering their own role and the impact they have are natural results of this disposition. Being compelled to create and contribute new and interesting ideas is also part of this disposition. This disposition of mind can be fostered and encouraged through intentional teaching at the beginning of school and is the ideal support for both learning and the development of the brain in early childhood.

I hope that these relationships between dispositions of mind, brain development, and early childhood education have inspired your own intellectual curiosity and creativity.

But now bear with me as I invite you to journey into the future, from early education to high school and college. I am now a parent of three teenage children, with one heading off to college, and I came upon an article by Christine Koh entitled, 'College Rejections Season Doesn't Have to Hurt This Much' (2022). As part of her research, Koh interviewed Julie Lythcott-Haims, former dean of freshman and undergraduate advising at Stanford University and asked about what she saw in students who thrived. Lythcott-Haims replied:

> Within the context of a culture that incentivizes students to go through rigorous motions to achieve narrow measures of success, the students who truly thrived were quirky, doing whatever it was their way. Even if they were doing something

on the well-beaten path, they knew who they were, what they wanted. They were humans with agency and they were going for it.

The students that are successful in this challenging and highly competitive college are those with an appreciation for knowledge-seeking as well as their contribution as an individual with purpose and impact.

Now, let's jump even further into the future and think about the likely job market for the next generation. Technology is developing at an exponential rate, and this changes the landscape of required skills. Companies are no longer hiring workers for their current skills; 'firms are looking for people who are flexible, who can present new ideas, inspire cooperation in groups, manage and lead teams' (Brackett, 2019). The qualities that make people fulfilled and successful in college and work are the same qualities I have described as beneficial dispositions of mind. A strong sense of self and motivation, and a disposition of mind towards learning, serves students well in early childhood, and will continue to serve them well in high school, and then in college and beyond.

There are parallels between the process of deepening knowledge and strengthening relationships on the neurological level and the lived experience level. Robust neural networks, needed for deep and flexible understanding, are the result of many connected and myelinated neurons. Likewise, the connections students forge with their peers and teachers are key contexts for learning. Connecting ideas and disciplines expands the depth and breadth of our knowledge. On both levels, we are talking about robust connections and the expansion of ideas and perspectives.

Learning and the corresponding neural changes in our brains are something we all have in common regardless of our age. Neuroplasticity is something that stays with us. Our strategies for encouraging and nurturing growth in our students are similar to those which will facilitate our *own* growth both professionally and as individuals. If one of the ultimate aims of education is to help children become the architects of their own learning both in school and beyond, we can do this by proactively expanding our own understanding.

The story of the beginning of education, early childhood, and the brain, is one that carries important implications for all of us individually and collectively well beyond schooling. Early childhood teacher/researchers should feel a sense of pride, for in taking seriously and sincerely the development of young children, we are helping to create beginnings for enduring impact.

ACKNOWLEDGMENTS

There are people who helped me in direct ways with this big project, by showing support and encouragement, and those that helped in indirect ways. Special thanks to Glenn Whitman and Sally Slater for the consistent encouragement you both gave me since I first mentioned the idea of writing this book. Each time you both asked me how my book was going, you gave me a little more 'juice' to get it done. Another special thanks to Mary Helen Immordino-Yang whose passion, intellect, and artistry has inspired me countless times before and during my year of writing. Thank you to Mary Helen for her generosity of spirit in agreeing to talk to me about these topics despite her busy schedule. I want to thank the other impressive educators who let me interview them for this book, Jennifer Azzariti and Perry Zurn. I often thought of one colleague in particular while writing this book, Peter Merrill. Peter Merrill was a dedicated educator and intellectual who showed kindness and wisdom to all; I am but one of the many who will miss you dearly. Thank you to Tom Carlson, who saw my potential and ignited a drive in me to understand more, to write more, to read more, and to give more. You exemplify a teacher whose passion is to help your students grow and find meaning in their lives; I am forever grateful, humbled and inspired by you. Thank you to Mark Combes from John Catt, for being a delight to work with, for answering my questions so promptly and efficiently, for being patient and humorous, and for making the process easy. Thank you to my editor, Anders Ingram for being so thoughtful as you shared your knowledge, wisdom, and perspective with me. Thank you to Denise Gershowitz for encouraging and supporting my grant work and my official entry into research in Mind, Brain, and Education. Thank you to my dear friends from early childhood to now, who have been part of my story and therefore also part of this book. Thank you to my parents and my sisters and brothers for being so supportive of me, always. And thank you once again, to my husband, Jonah, who took more than his fair share of driving kids around and cooking dinners these last two years! Thank you, Jonah, Stella, Sheldon, Owen, and Eli whom I love with all my heart and soul. You make everything possible.

BIBLIOGRAPHY

Aamodt, S. and S. Wang (2011) *Welcome To Your Child's Brain: How the mind grows from conception to college.*

Aguliar, Elena (2018) *Onward: Cultivating emotional resilience in educators.*

Alain, Émile Chartier (1932) *Propos sur l'éducation.*

Allee-Herndon, K. A., Taylor, D. D., and S. K. Roberts (2019) "Putting play in its place: Presenting a continuum to decrease mental health referrals and increase purposeful play in classrooms". *International Journal of Play*, 8:2, 186-203.

Barker, J., Michaelson, L., Munakata, Y., Provan, L. S., Semenov, A. D., and H. R. Synder (2014) "Less Structured Times in Children's Daily Lives Predicts Self-directed Executive Functioning", *Frontiers in Psychology* 5. Available at: https://doi.org/10.3389/fpsyg.2014.00593.

Baumeister, R. F. and J. Tierney (2011) "Breaker of Rocks", *Smithsonian Magazine*, December 2011, 78-86.

Bending, M. and A. E. Devercelli (2022) *Quality Early Learning: Nurturing Children's Potential.*

Bendini, Magdalena, and A. E. Devercelli (eds) (2022) *Quality Early Learning: Nurturing children's potential, human development perspectives.* Available at: https://openknowledge.worldbank.org/entities/publication/fbf3b572-91e6-5c13-89af-334fab423621.

Berger, Warren (2014) *A More Beautiful Question: The power of inquiry to spark breakthrough ideas.*

Beveridge, W. I. B. (1957) *The Art of Scientific Investigation.*

Bird, K. and M. J. Sherwin (2006) *American Prometheus: The triumph and tragedy of J. Robert Oppenheimer.*

Bodrova, E. and D. J. Leong (2007) *Tools of the Mind: The Vygotskian approach to early childhood education.*

Borba, M. (2021) *Thrivers: The surprising reasons why some kids struggle and others shine.*

Bowen, Jose Antonio (2021) *Teaching Change: How to develop independent thinkers using relationships, resilience, and reflection.*

Brackett, Marc (2019) *Permission to Feel: The power of emotional intelligence to achieve well-being and success.*

Bronfenbrenner, Urie (1979) *The Ecology of Human Development.*

Bronk, K. C., and W. Damon (2022) "Scientific and Ethical Mandates in the Study of Purpose". *Human Development*, 66:3, 219-221.

Bronson, P. and Merryman, A. (2010) *Nurture Shock: New thinking about children.*

Brown, P. C., Roediger III, H. L., and M. A. McDaniel (2014) *Make It Stick: The science of successful learning.*

Buchsbaum, D., Bridgers, S., Skolnick, Weisberg D., and A. Gopnik (2012) "The Power of Possibility: Causal learning, counterfactual reasoning, and pretend play". *Philosophical Transactions of the Royal Society B Biological Sciences.* 5:367, 2202-12. DOI: 10.1098/rstb.2012.0122.

Bull, R., Espy, K. A., and S. A. Wiebe (2008) "Short-Term Memory, Working Memory, and Executive Functioning in Preschoolers: Longitudinal predictors of mathematical achievement at age 7 years". *Developmental Neuropsychology.* 33:3, 205-28. DOI: 10.1080/87565640801982312.

Bunge, S. A., Dudukovic, N. M., Thomason, M. E., Vaidya, C. J., and J. D. Gabrieli (2002) "Immature Frontal Lobe Contributions to Cognitive Control in Children: Evidence from fMRI". *Neuron.* 33:2, 301-11. DOI: 10.1016/s0896-6273(01)00583-9.

Cadwell, L. B. (1997) *Bringing Reggio Emilia Home: An innovative approach to early childhood education.*

Cantor, Pamela, Lerner, Richard M., Pittman, Karen J., Case, Paul A. and Nora Gomberts (2021) *Whole-Child Development, Learning and Thriving: A dynamic systems approach.*

Carson, Rachel, (1965) *The Sense of Wonder.*

Chouinard, M. M. (2007) "Children's Questions: A Mechanism for Cognitive Development." *Monographs of the Society for Research in Child Development.* 72:1, vii-ix, 1-112.

Christakis, Erika (2016) *The Importance of Being Little: What preschoolers really need from grownups.*

Clark, C. A. C., Pritchard, V. E., and L. J. Woodward (2010) "Preschool executive functioning abilities predict early mathematics achievement". *Developmental Psychology.* 46:5, 1176-1191. DOI: 10.1037/a0019672.

Comalli, D. M., Keen, R., Abraham, E. S., Foo, V. J., Lee, M.-H., and K. E. Adolph (2016) "The Development of Tool Use: Planning for end-state comfort". *Developmental Psychology,* 52:11, 1878-1892. DOI: 10.1037/dev0000207.

Csikszentmihalyi, M. (2009) *Flow: The Psychology of Optimal Experience.*

Darling-Hammond, L., and Snyder, J. (2000) "Authentic assessment of teaching in context". *Teaching and Teacher Education,* 16:5-6, 523-545.

Dehaene, S. (2009) *Reading in the Brain: The new science of how we read.*

Dehaene, S. (2011) *The Number Sense: How the mind creates mathematics.*

Dehaene, S. (2020) *How We Learn: Why brains learn better than any machine … for now.*

Demasio, Antonio (2012). "Emotions Create Our Preferences: The somatic marker hypothesis", *NeuroRelay,* Available at: http://neurorelay.com/2012/05/15/emotions-create-our-preferences-the-somatic-marker-hypothesis/.

Dewey, John (1897) "My Pedagogic Creed". *School Journal,* 54:3, 77-80.

DeYoung, C. G. (2013) "The Neuromodulator of Exploration: A unifying theory of the role of dopamine in personality". *Frontiers in Human Neuroscience* 7:762. DOI: 10.3389/fnhum.2013.00762.

Diamond, A. (2013) "Executive functions". *Annual Review of Psychology.* 64, 135-68. DOI: 10.1146/annurev-psych-113011-143750.

Diamond, A., and D. S. Ling, (2020) 'Review of the evidence on, and fundamental questions about, efforts to improve executive functions, including working memory', in J. M. Novick, M. F. Bunting, M. R. Dougherty, and R. W. Engle (eds.) *Cognitive and Working Memory Training: Perspectives from psychology, neuroscience, and human development,* 143-431.

Dunfield, K. A., and V. A. Kuhlmeier (2010) "Intention-mediated selective helping in infancy". *Psychological Science*. 21:4, 523-527. DOI: 10.1177/0956797610364119.

Duval, P. E., Fornari, E., Decaillet, M., Ledoux, J. B., Beaty, R. E. and S. Denervaud (2023) "Creative Thinking and Brain Network Development in Schoolchildren". *Developmental Science*. 26:6 DOI: 10.1111/desc.13389.

Dweck, C. S. (2007) *Mindset: The new psychology of success.*

Edwards, C., Gandini, L. and G. Forman (1998) *The Hundred Languages of Children: The Reggio Emilia Approach.*

Edwards, C. P., and L. Gandini (2015) "Teacher Research in Reggio Emilia, Italy: Essence of a dynamic, evolving role." *Voices of Practitioners: Teacher research in early childhood education*, 10:1. Available at: https://digitalcommons.unl.edu/famconfacpub/105/.

Einstein, Albert (1954) 'Society and Personality: *Mein Weltbild*, 1934 (excerpt)' in *Ideas and Opinions*, ed. Carl Seelig, trs. Sonja Bargmann.

Einstein, Albert (1954) 'Testimonial for An Essay on the Psychology of Invention in the Mathematical Field by Jacques S. Hadamard, Princeton University Press, 1945' in *Ideas and Opinions*, ed. Carl Seelig, trs. Sonja Bargmann.

Eisenberg N., and T. L. Spinrad (2004) "Emotion-Related Regulation: Sharpening the definition". *Child Development*. 75:2, 334-9. DOI: 10.1111/j.1467-8624.2004.00674.x.

Eisner, Elliot W. (2002) *The Arts and the Creation of Mind.*

Eliot, Lise (2008) *What's Going On in There? How the brain and mind develop in the first five years of life.*

Elkind, David (2007) *The Power of Play: Learning what comes naturally.*

Engel, Susan, (2020) 'Why Should This Be So? The Waxing and Waning of Children's Curiosity', in *Curiosity Studies: A New Ecology of Knowledge*, edited by Perry Zurn and Arjun Shankar.

Engel, Susan (2021) *The Intellectual Lives of Children.*

Engel, S. and K. Randall (2009) "How Teachers Respond to Children's Inquiry" *American Education Research Journal*, 46:1. DOI: 10.3102/0002831208323274.

Farran, Dale C. (2022) 'Early Developmental Competencies: Or Why Pre-K Does Not Have Lasting Effects', *Defending the Early Years*, Available at: https://dey.org/early-developmental-competencies-or-why-pre-k-does-not-have-lasting-effects/.

Fiske, A., and K. Holmboe (2019) "Neural Substrates of Early Executive Function Development." *Developmental Review* 52, 42-62.

Follmer, D. J. (2018). "Executive function and reading comprehension: A meta-analytic review". *Educational Psychologist*. 53:1, 42-60. DOI: 10.1080/00461520.2017.1309295.

Freire, Paulo (1998) *Pedagogy of Freedom: Ethics, democracy, and civic courage.*

Frenzel, A. C., Goetz, T., Lüdtke, O., Pekrun, R., and R. E. Sutton (2009) "Emotional Transmission in the Classroom: Exploring the relationship between teacher and student enjoyment." *Journal of Educational Psychology*, 101:3, 705-716.

Frenzel, A. C., Becker-Kurz, B., Pekrun, R., Goetz, T., and O. Lüdtke (2018). "Emotional Transmission in the Classroom Revisited: A reciprocal effects model of teacher and student enjoyment". *Journal of Educational Psychology*, 110:5, 628–639.

Gagnier, K. M., and K. R. Fisher (2020) "Unpacking the Black Box of Translation: A framework for infusing spatial thinking into curricula." *Cognitive Research: Principles and Implications* 5:1, 1-19.

Gagnier, K. and N. Newcombe (2021) 'Spatial Enhancements to boost Learning of Science and Mathematics', *International Bureau of Education Blog*, Available at: https://solportal.ibe-unesco.org/spatial-enhancements-to-boost-learning-of-science-and-math/.

Galinsky, Ellen. (2011) *Mind in the Making: The seven essential life skills every child needs.*

Gardner, H. (1990) *Art Education and Human Development.*

Goldenberg, Claude (2021) 'The Science of Reading Should Make Room for Skepticism (Just Not for Ignorance)'. *Edweek*. Available at: https://www.edweek.org/teaching-learning/opinion-the-science-of-reading-should-make-room-for-skepticism-just-not-for-ignorance/2021/09.

Golinkoff, R. M., and K. Hirsh-Pasek (2016) *Becoming Brilliant: What science tells us about raising successful children.*

Gopnik, Alison (2017) *The Gardener and the Carpenter: What the new science of child development tells us about the relationship between parents and children.*

Gopnik, A. (2011) 'Why Preschool Shouldn't be Like School.' *Slate*. Available at: https://slate.com/human-interest/2011/03/preschool-lessons-new-research-shows-that-teaching-kids-more-and-more-at-ever-younger-ages-may-backfire.html.

Gotlieb, R. J. M, Immordino-Yang, M. H., Gonzalez, E., Reinhart, L., Mahjouri, S., Pueschel, E. and G. Nadaya (2022) "Becoming Literate: Educational Implications of Coordinated Neuropsychological Development of Reading and Social-Emotional Functioning Among Diverse Youth". *Literacy Research: Theory, Method, and Practice*. 71:1. Available at: https://doi.org/10.1177/23813377221120107.

Gotlieb, R., Yang, X., and M. H. Immordino-Yang (2023) "Diverse Adolescents' Transcendent Thinking Predicts Young Adult Psychosocial Outcomes via Brain Network Development". *PsyArXiv*. DOI: 10.31234/osf.io/cj6an.

Gottlieb, S., Keltner, D. and T. Lambrozo (2018) "Awe As a Scientific Emotion" *Cognitive Science* 42:6. DOI: 10.1111/cogs.12648.

Gough, P. B., and W. E. Tunmer (1986) "Decoding, Reading, and Reading Disability". *Remedial and Special Education*, 7:1, 6-10.

Gray, Peter (2013) *Free to Learn: Why unleashing the instinct to play will make our children happier, more self-reliant, and better students for life.*

Hart, B. and T. R. Risley (1995) *Meaningful Difference in Everyday Experience of Young American Children.*

Hattie, J. and K. Zierer (2018) *10 Mindframes for Visible Learning: Teaching for success.*

Healey, Jane M. (2004) *Your Child's Growing Mind: Brain development and learning from birth to adolescent.*

Heilman, Kenneth M. (2016) "Possible Brain Mechanisms of Creativity". *Archives of Clinical Neuropsychology*. 31, 285-296.

Hopkins, Rob (2018) 'Kyung Hee Kim on 'The Creativity Crisis". Available at: https://www.robhopkins.net/2018/09/20/kyung-hee-kim-on-the-creativity-crisis/.

Hopkins, Rob (2019) *From What Is to What If: Unleashing the power of imagination to create the future we want.*

Hooks, Bell (1996) *Killing Rage: Ending racism.*

Hoover, W. A., and W. E. Tunmer (2018). "The Simple View of Reading: Three assessments of its adequacy". *Remedial and Special Education*, 39:5, 304-312.

Hurston, Z. N., and C. Kaplan (ed.) (2003) *Zora Neal Hurston: A Life in Letters.*

Immordino-Yang, M. H. (2016) *Emotions, Learning, and The Brain: Exploring the educational implications of affective neuroscience.*

Immordino-Yang, M. H., and A. Demasio (2007). "We Feel, Therefore We Learn: The relevance of affective and social neuroscience to education". *Mind, Brain, and Education*, 1:1, 3-10.

Immordino-Yang, M. H. and K. Fischer (2008) *The Jossey-Bass Reader on the Brain and Learning.*

Immordino-Yang, M. H., Darling-Hammond, L, and C. Krone (2018) *The Brain Basis for Integrated Social, Emotional, and Academic Development: How emotions and social relationships drive learning*, Aspen Institute, September 20. Available at: https://www.aspeninstitute.org/publications/the-brain-basis-for-integrated-social-emotional-and-academic-development/.

Immordino-Yang, M. H., D. R. Knecht (2020) 'Building Meaning Builds Teens Brains', *ASCD*, May 1. 77. Available at https://www.ascd.org/el/articles/building-meaning-builds-teens-brains.

Joldersma, Clarence and Jo Herwegen (2022). 'Contexts of educational neuroscience' in *Reimagining Education: The International Science and Evidence based Education Assessment*. DOI: 10.56383/RUNC9656.

Kamenetz, Anya (2022) 'A Top Researcher Says It's Time to Rethink Our Entire Approach to Preschool', *NPR Education*. Available at: https://www.npr.org/2022/02/10/1079406041/researcher-says-rethink-prek-preschool-prekindergarten.

Kaufman, S. B., Singer, J., and D. G. Singer (2013) 'The Need for Pretend Play in Child Development', *Scientific American Blog*. Available at: https://blogs.scientificamerican.com/beautiful-minds/the-need-for-pretend-play-in-child-development/

Kaufman, Scott Barry and Carolyn Gregoire (2015) *Wired to Create: Unraveling the Mysteries of the Creative Mind.*

Kelley, Tom and David Kelley (2012) 'Reclaim Your Creative Confidence', *Harvard Business Review.*

Keltner, Dacher (2023) *Awe: The new science of everyday wonder and how it can transform your life.*

Kierkegaard, Soren (1859) *The Point of View for My Work as an Author.*

Kim, K. H. (2016) *The Creativity Challenge: How we can recapture American innovation.*

Koh, C. (2022) 'College Rejections Season Doesn't Have to Hurt This Much: We need to rethink the college admissions rat race'. *The Boston Globe.* Available at: https://www.bostonglobe.com/2022/02/23/magazine/college-rejection-season-doesnt-have-hurt-this-much/.

Krechevsky, M., Mardell, B., Rivard, M., and D. Wilson (2013) *Visible Learners: Promoting Reggio-inspired approaches in all schools.*

Lewin-Benham, A. (2011) *Twelve Best Practices for Early Childhood Education: Integrating Reggio and other inspired approaches.*

Lieberman, Matthew D. (2013) *Social: Why our brains are wired to connect.*

Lillard, A. S., and R. D. Kavanaugh (2014) "The Contribution of Symbolic Skills to the Development of an Explicit Theory of Mind". *Child Development*, 85:4, 1535-1551.

Lone, Jana Mohr (2021) 'Philosophy with Children' *Aeon.* Available at: https://aeon.co/essays/how-to-do-philosophy-for-and-with-children.

Mader, Jackie (2022) 'A State-Funded Pre-k Program Let to 'Significantly Negative Effects' for Kids In Tennessee'. *The Hechinger Report.* Available at: https://hechingerreport.org/a-state-funded-pre-k-program-led-to-significantly-negative-effects-for-kids-in-tennessee/.

Magsamen, Susan and Ivy Ross (2023) *Your Brain on Art: How the arts transform us.*

Malin, H., Liauw, I., and W. Damon (2017) "Purpose and Character Development in Early Adolescence". *Journal of Youth and Adolescence.* 46:6, 1200-1215.

McCullough, D. (2016) *The Wright Brothers.*

Medina, John (2010) *Brain Rules for Baby: How to raise a smart happy child from zero to five.*

Murray, Carol Garboden (2017) 'The Invisible Curriculum of Care.' *Caring Rituals* July/August. Available from: https://exchangepress.com/.

Newkirk, Thomas (2015) 'On The Virtue of Thinking Small: Reclaiming teacher research' in Glover, M., and E. O. Keene (eds.) *The Teacher You Want to Be: Essays about children, learning, and teaching.*

Osher, D., Cantor, P., Berg, J., Steyer, L., and T. Rose (2020) "Drivers of human development: How relationships and context shape learning and development". *Applied Developmental Science*, 24:1, 6-36.

Ostroff, Wendy L. (2012) *Understanding How Young Children Learn: Bringing the science of child development to the classroom.*

Patall, Eirka A. and Jeanette Zambrano (2019) "Facilitating Student Outcomes by Supporting Autonomy: Implication for Practice and Policy". *Policy Insights from the Behavioral and Brain Sciences.* 6:2, 115-122.

Pyle, Angela and Erica Danniels (2016). "A Continuum of Play-Based Learning: The Role of the Teacher in Play-Based Pedagogy and the Fear of Hijacking Play". *Early Education and Development*, 1-16. DOI: 10.1080/10409289.2016.1220771.

Resnick, Mitchel (2017) *Lifelong Kindergarten: Cultivating creativity through projects, passion, peers, and play.*

Rinaldi, C. (2012) 'The Pedagogy of Listening: The Listening Perspective from Reggio Emilia' in *The Hundred Languages of Children: The Reggio Emilia Approach in Transformation*, 3rd ed, eds. C. P. Edwards, Gandini, L. and G. Forman, 233-246.

Rodriguez, Vanessa and Michelle Fitzpatrick (2014) *The Teaching Brain: An evolutionary trait at the heart of education.*

Romeo, R. R., Leonard, J. A., Robinson, S. T., West, M. R., Mackey, A. P., Rowe, M. L., and J. D. E. Gabrieli (2018). "Beyond the 30-Million-Word Gap: Children's Conversational Exposure Is Associated With Language-Related Brain Function". *Psychological Science*, 29:5, 700-710. Available at: https://doi.org/10.1177/0956797617742725.

Rose, T. (2016) *The End of Average: How We Succeed in a World that Values Sameness.*

Ryan, R. M., and E. L. Deci (2017) *Self-Determination Theory: Basic psychological needs in motivation, development, and wellness.*

Seigel, D., and T. P. Bryson (2011) *The Whole-Brain Child: 12 Strategies to Nurture Your Child's Developing Mind.*

Seigel, D. (2020) *The Developing Mind: How relationships and the brain interact to shape who we are.*

Seo, K. H., and H. P. Ginsburg (2004). 'What Is Developmentally Appropriate in Early Childhood Mathematics Education?' in D. H. Clements, & J. Sarama (Eds.), *Engaging Young Children in Mathematics*, 91-104.

Shiota, M., Kelter, D. and A. Mossman, (2007) "The Nature of Awe: Elicitors, Appraisals, and Effects on Self-Concept", *Cognition and Emotion*, 21:5. DOI:10.1080/02699930600923668.

Shonkoff, J. P., et al (2011) *Building the Brain's 'Air Traffic Control' System: How early experiences shape the development of executive function.* Working paper 11. National Scientific Council on the Developing Child. Center on the Developing Child Harvard University. Avaliable at: https://harvardcenter. wpenginepowered.com/wp-content/uploads/2011/05/How-Early-Experiences-Shape-the-Development-of-Executive-Function.pdf.

Shonkoff, J. P., et al, 'Connecting the Brain to the Rest of the Body: Early Childhood Development and Lifelong Health Are Deeply Intertwined' (2020), National Scientific Council on the Developing Child, Working Paper 15. Available at: https://harvardcenter.wpenginepowered.com/wp-content/uploads/2020/06/wp15_health_FINALv2.pdf.

Singer, E. (2013) "Play and Playfulness: basic features of early childhood education", *European Early Childhood Education Research Journal*, 21:2, 172-184, DOI: 10.1080/1350293X.2013.789198.

Singer, D. G., Golinkoff, R. M., and K. Hirsh-Pasek (Eds.) (2006) *Play = Learning: How play motivates and enhances children's cognitive and social-emotional growth.*

Spelke, E. and K. Shutts (2020) 'Learning in the Early Years' in Bendini, M. and A. E. Devercelli (eds.) *Quality Early Learning: Nurturing children's potential.*

Stamm, Jill (2007) *Bright From the Start: The simple, science-backed way to nuruture your child's developing mind from birth to age 3.*

Stonvich, K., (1986) "Matthew Effects in Reading: Some Consequences of Individual Differences in the Acquisition of Literacy". *Reading Research Quarterly*, 21:4, 360-407.

Sylva, K., Melhuish, E., Sammons, P., Siraj, I., and B. Taggart (2004) *The Effective Provision of Pre-School Education (EPPE) Project Technical Paper 12: The Final Report - Effective Pre-School Education.* A Longitudinal Study Funded by the DfES 1997-2004. Available at: https://dera.ioe.ac.uk/id/eprint/18189/2/SSU-SF-2004-01.pdf.

Terada, Y. (2022) 'We Drastically Underestimate the Importance of Brain Breaks: When it comes to optimizing learning, we don't value break enough, neuroscientist suggest in a new study'. *Edutopia*. Available at: https://www.edutopia.org/article/we-drastically-underestimate-importance-brain-breaks/.

Tokuhama-Espinosa, Tracey (2018) *Neuromyths: Debunking false ideas about the brain.*

Tomasello, Michael (2019) *Becoming Human: A theory of ontogeny.*

Vaish, A., Carpenter, M., and M. Tomasello (2010) "Young children selectively avoid helping people with harmful intentions". *Child Development.* 81:6, 1661-1669. DOI: 10.1111/j.1467-8624.2010.01500.x.

Vecchi, Vea (2010) *Art and Creativity in Reggio Emilia: Exploring the role and potential of ateliers in early childhood education.*

Verdine, B., Golinkoff, R. M., Hirsh-Pasek, K, Newcombe, N., Filipwicz, A. T., and A. Change (2013) "Deconstructing Building Blocks: Preschoolers Spatial Assembly Performance Relates to Early Math Skills", *Child Development*, May, 85:3, 1062-1076

Waldinger R. and M. Schulz (2023) *The Good Life: Lessons from the world's longest scientific study of happiness.*

Walton, G. (2021). 'Stop Telling Students, 'You Belong!': 3 ways to make a sense of belonging real and valuable.' *EdWeek*, November 09, 2021. Available at: https://www.edweek.org/leadership/opinion-stop-telling-students-you-belong/2021/11.

Wells, G. (2009) *The Meaning Makers: Learning to talk and talking to learn.*

Whitman, Glenn and Ian Kelleher (2016) *Neuroteach: Brain science and the future of education.*

Whitebread, D. and Y. Sitabkhan (2020) 'Pedagogy and Curricula Content: Building Foundational Skills and Knowledge.' In *Quality Early Learning: Nurturing Children's Potential.* Edited by Bendini, M. and A. E. Devercelli, 83-116.

Willingham, D. T. (2017) *The Reading Mind: A cognitive approach to understanding how the mind reads.*

Willis, Judy (2006) *Research-Based Strategies to Ignite Student Learning.*

Willis, Judy (2008) *How Your Child Learns Best.*

Willis, Judy (2010) *Mind, Brain, and Education: Neuroscience implications for the classroom.*

Woo, B. M., and E. S. Spelke (2023) "Toddlers' Social Evaluations of Agents Who Act on False beliefs" *Developmental Science.* 26:e13314. DOI: 10.1111/desc.13314.

Wurman, Richard Saul, (2014) 'Information architect for the world's greatest cities', *Business Innovation factory.* Available at: https://www.youtube.com/watch?v=2pVz67Pn7gU.

Zurn, Perry, and Dani S. Bassett (2022) *Curious Minds: The power of connection.*